SCIENTIFIC AMERICAN EXPLORES BIG IDEAS

The Science of Food

The Editors of *Scientific American*

SCIENTIFIC AMERICAN | EDUCATIONAL PUBLISHING

New York

Published in 2026 by Scientific American Educational Publishing
in association with **The Rosen Publishing Group**
2544 Clinton Street, Buffalo NY 14224

Contains material from Scientific American®, a division of Springer Nature America, Inc., reprinted by permission, as well as original material from The Rosen Publishing Group®.

First Edition

Scientific American
Lisa Pallatroni: Project Editor

Rosen Publishing
Danielle Haynes: Compiling Editor
Michael Moy: Senior Graphic Designer

Cataloging-in-Publication Data

Names: Scientific American, Inc.
Title: The science of food / edited by the Scientific American Editors.
Description: Buffalo, New York : Scientific American Educational Publishing, an imprint of Rosen Publishing, 2026. | Series: Scientific American explores big ideas | Includes glossary and index.
Identifiers: ISBN 9781538313169 (pbk.) | ISBN 9781538313176 (library bound) | ISBN 9781538313183 (ebook)
Subjects: LCSH: Food–Research–Juvenile literature. | Food industry and trade–Juvenile literature.
Classification: LCC TX355.S356 2026 | DDC 664–dc23

Manufactured in the United States of America
Websites listed were live at the time of publication.

Cover: JGalione/istock.com

CPSIA Compliance Information: Batch # CSSA26.
For Further Information contact Rosen Publishing at 1-800-237-9932.

CONTENTS

INTRODUCTION

When you think about the essential things we need as humans to live, there are usually three things at the top of the list: air, water, and food. The latter is, arguably, both the most enjoyable and controversial. Food is necessary, yes, but it's also in shortage for millions of people, a source of creativity for others, and, across the globe, a multi-trillion-dollar industry.

But what about the science of food? Tens of thousands of years ago, humans began cultivating food, selecting plants for their best qualities–nutrition, taste, and ease of growing. Today, scientists do the same in the lab, using new technology to alter the genes of our favorite foodstuffs and even creating lab-grown meat.

The articles in this book will delve deeper into the science of food and human behavior as it relates to it. In Section 1, "Exploring Our Food Past," we take a look at some of the ways our ancestors kept themselves fed and explored the ingredients available to them. Section 2, "Cravings and Taste," examines why people love the taste of some foods more than others and how the brain can create food addictions. Further exploring the human body, Section 3, "Nutrition and Health," addresses the almighty link between what you eat and how it makes you feel. How scientists use technology to make safer, healthier, and better-tasting food takes center stage in Section 4. And in Section 5, "The Food Industry's Impact on the Environment," we look at ways to reduce food waste, plastic packaging, and the overall impact the food industry has on the Earth and climate.

Section 1: Exploring Our Food Past

The Surprising Story of How Peaches Became an Icon of the U.S. Southeast

By Meghan Bartels

The fuzzy, sweet stone fruit traces back to China, where it has been cultivated for more than 8,000 years. It wasn't until the 1500s that Spanish colonists carried peaches into the Americas when they first explored the North American Southeast, where the fruit gained a foothold in what is now Georgia. Scientists have known that much about this symbol of summer. But how did peaches become so widespread in the U.S.? Research published in September in *Nature Communications* argues that after the fruit was introduced by Europeans, the peach spread across much of what is now the eastern U.S. with the help of Indigenous peoples.

"Today, Georgia is the Peach State," says botanist RaeLynn Butler, secretary of culture and humanities at the Muscogee (Creek) Nation and a co-author of the new research. "That legacy stems from a long history." Much of that history comes from the Muscogee (Creek) Nation and other Indigenous communities that lived in the area when peaches first arrived in the Americas.

"A lot of choices and agency by Indigenous people played a huge role," says Jacob Holland-Lulewicz, an archaeologist at Pennsylvania State University and a co-author of the new research. They "were also responsible for structuring the ecology and the landscape to be an appropriate place for peaches to grow, and they tended to the peach plants."

Holland-Lulewicz had long noted reports of peach pits found at archaeological sites across the southeastern U.S. And a few years ago he decided to compile these into a more detailed picture of how peaches spread–one that could shed light on the Indigenous histories that archaeology has typically ignored or suppressed. "I started to think about [the fruit] as a trade good," he says. "Maybe we could use peaches to track, at a really high resolution, how Indigenous communities were interacting."

The research team gathered evidence from more than two dozen archaeological sites and several early towns across the southeastern U.S. where one or more peaches had been discovered. Previous research at some of these sites had already provided a time frame for the presence of peaches. For the sites where that age had not yet been determined, the researchers used radiocarbon dating, either directly on peach pits or on other nearby materials to establish when peaches were likely present.

This work, however, showed only where peach pits had survived–not how people used the fruit or seeds. "We can't see what people actually did with peaches and peach pits, so we're making inferences based on the archaeological record," says Kristen Gremillion, an archaeobotanist at the Ohio State University, who has researched peach history in the Americas but was not involved in the new research.

Perhaps the most surprising date the study authors determined comes from a site in inland Georgia, where Ancestral Muskogean people lived for a few decades beginning in the early to mid-1500s. The researchers suggest that the two peach pits found at this site may be related to Hernando de Soto's early expedition inland in 1540, one of a series of journeys that bands of Spaniards made during their first century in the Americas.

Beyond this outlier, the peach pits didn't appear to reach inland Georgia until decades later. The bulk of early peaches, dating to before 1600, come from coastal Florida and Georgia. The fruit then spread across a swath of northern Florida and southern Georgia between 1625 and 1640. By 1650, peaches had moved throughout the rest of Georgia and eastern Alabama, plus some sites in North Carolina and eastern Tennessee. The fruit had reached Arkansas by the 1670s, the researchers found, and prior archaeological records show peaches arriving in New York State before the beginning of the 18th century.

The pattern struck Holland-Lulewicz and his co-authors as both surprising and telling. The Spanish pivoted from occasional expeditions to putting down roots in the Southeast beginning in the 1560s, and only then did peaches appear to do the same. But throughout the time of the great peach migration, most Europeans in North America were still concentrated in small population centers along the coasts. The fruit's spread vastly outpaced Spanish colonization, suggesting that Indigenous people, not Spanish explorers and conquistadors, did the work.

"This spread really started when Indigenous networks and Spanish networks were starting to be entangled with one another," Holland-Lulewicz says. "From there, peaches are being spread through the rest of the Indigenous networks to communities and towns that may have never even, still, met a Spanish person."

Given how quickly peach pits spread and how long it takes peach trees to bear fruit, he says, Indigenous peoples must have transferred them along existing networks. "This land was a continent of active sociopolitical entities and communities and nations," Holland-Lulewicz says. "These relationships created this entire continental web of interaction. These were not disconnected people living in the forest."

From Butler's experience as both a botanist and a member of the Muscogee (Creek) nation, the findings are no surprise. Her ancestors lived across what is now Alabama, Georgia, Florida and South Carolina until the 1830s, when the U.S. Army brutally forced Indigenous nations of the Southeast westward to Oklahoma in what is often referred to as the Trail of Tears.

The Muscogee (Creek) Nation's connection with peaches survived the trauma, a testament to the importance of the crop to its members' lives in the U.S. East. For example, the nation included the ripening of peaches among the timekeeping milestones it saw in the natural world, Butler says. Her hereditary tribal town, Pakan Tallahassee, was named for peaches, and she says these ancestors would have shared the fruit with other communities and taken care of the trees–no small feat, she notes. "You've got to be determined and patient," Butler says.

Indigenous peoples would have been well-equipped to cultivate peaches from experience with other tree crops such as pawpaws and chestnuts, Holland-Lulewicz says. And Indigenous practices such as controlled burns would have created open landscapes that favored sun-loving plants such as peaches.

The U.S. Indian Removal Act of the 1830s uprooted Indigenous nations, including Butler's ancestors, who carried peach pits on the long journey west and still tend trees in Oklahoma. Back in the East, peach trees suddenly left untended sometimes became too overgrown to bear much fruit. Others survived on farmsteads, where their fruit was fed to pigs or turned into cider, says William Thomas Okie, a historian at Kennesaw State University, who has written about peaches but was not involved in the new research.

Despite the historical importance of peaches across the eastern U.S., the modern peach industry that began in the late 1800s is linked to a separate introduction of a specific large, attractive variety from Asia called the Chinese Cling, Okie says. But some of the commercialized cultivars may have mixed the Chinese Cling and other later arrivals with the peach varieties grown by Indigenous breeders across the southeastern U.S. before their eviction, he says.

Butler hopes future research will examine different peach varieties–particularly those her nation continues to grow in Oklahoma–and determine whether they are genetically related to the first fruits Indigenous groups spread across the eastern U.S. "It's just neat to see science in action and how it applies to everyday life," she says. "Everyone has enjoyed a peach at some point in their life but maybe never thought about how it got here."

About the Author

Meghan Bartels is a science journalist based in New York City. She joined Scientific American *in 2023 and is now a senior news reporter there. Previously, she spent more than four years as a writer and editor at Space.com, as well as nearly a year as a science reporter at* Newsweek, *where she focused on space and Earth science. Her writing has also appeared in* Audubon, Nautilus, Astronomy *and* Smithsonian, *among other publications. She attended Georgetown University and earned a master's degree in journalism at New York University's Science, Health and Environmental Reporting Program.*

1,800-Year-Old Spices Are Earliest Evidence of Curry Making in Southeast Asia

By O. Rose Broderick

Dishes that are rich in flavor and aroma from combinations of spices such as earthy turmeric, warm cloves and sharp ginger—commonly known as curries in the West—have starred in cuisines throughout South and Southeast Asia, from India to Indonesia, for centuries. Not all the spices used in each place are native to that spot, though, which points to a robust ancient spice trade. But how ancient those culinary traditions are, where they originated, and how far the spices traveled are questions archaeologists have long been trying to answer.

New evidence of the use of nonnative spices, found during an archaeological excavation in what is today southern Vietnam, pushes back the arrival of these spices and culinary traditions into Southeast Asia by hundreds of years, according to a study published on Friday in *Science Advances*. Archaeologists found microscopic fragments of spices such as cinnamon (native to Sri Lanka) and nutmeg (native to the tiny Banda Islands in eastern Indonesia) beaten into sandstone tools at the Óc Eo excavation site southwest of present-day Ho Chi Minh City.

"They mentioned spices like cloves, and cloves come from one specific group of islands in eastern Indonesia," says Tom Hoogervorst, a linguist and archaeologist at the Royal Netherlands Institute of Southeast Asian and Caribbean Studies, who was not involved with the new research. "The moment you find them in a different context, then you know that people were doing long-term sailing—basically a maritime network."

Historians have long known about a maritime trade route that ran during the same era as the famed Silk Road, a network of land routes between the Mediterranean Sea and China. The maritime route went farther south, connecting cultures in what is today Iran, India and Southeast Asia. But most of the evidence comes from written records, and the lack of physical evidence has made it difficult for researchers to verify these accounts.

"Before this study, we had only limited clues from ancient documents in India, China and Rome about the early spice trades," says Australian National University archaeologist and study co-author Hsiao-chun Hung. "However, this research is the first to confirm that these spices were indeed traded commodities that existed within the global maritime trading networks nearly 2,000 years ago."

Though previous fragments found elsewhere predate the third- and fourth-century C.E. spices analyzed in the new study, the Óc Eo findings offer the first evidence that these spices were all used in Southeast Asia during this time period. The spice remains indicate that the stone mortars, pestles and grinding slabs found there were likely used for food preparation.

Traces of eight spices were found: turmeric, ginger, fingerroot, sand ginger, galangal, clove, nutmeg and cinnamon. (One nutmeg fragment even retained a faint version of its signature pungent, slightly nutty aroma.) Because most of these spices originated on distant islands, traders would have had to bring them from several thousand kilometers away by sea. Hung says the stone tools were also likely imported, which suggests the larger culinary practice of incorporating such spices into foods was also borrowed from another ancient culture. "This study reveals that trading activities were rather complicated, as not only precious goods were moving around, but also people and their entire set of culinary cultures were transferred between the regions," she says.

First excavated in the 1940s, Óc Eo has been a fruitful site for archaeologists. The current study is part of a larger project conducted by the Vietnam Academy of Social Sciences to unearth more of the region's largely unknown ancient history. Chinese historical documents contain some records of an empire centered in what is now southern Vietnam that spanned Southeast Asia and disappeared by the seventh century C.E. Physical evidence of this kingdom is scarce, however.

This lack partly stems from rot caused by the area's humid, tropical climate, Hoogervorst says. "It's really tough to find the remains of food items in an archaeological assemblage," he says. "What [the researchers] were able to do, it's a good contribution to the history of food in Southeast Asia."

But Hoogervorst adds that it's a stretch to assume the stone grinding tools found at Óc Eo were also imported from distant areas. "To assume that people in Southeast Asia couldn't figure out how to basically crush their food with these stones is a huge leap," he says.

Hoogervorst is also skeptical that these ancient culinary traditions stem solely from South Asia. Given that many of the involved spices originate across the Asian continent–not just South Asia–he suggests it was more of an exchange than a unidirectional flow of culinary traditions. The study authors contend that the South Asian ornaments, pottery vessels and religious monuments excavated alongside the starch grains, date from a similar time and increase the likelihood that these culinary practices stem from South Asia and not somewhere nearby.

Other experts want to see the use of additional methods to establish chronology because radiocarbon dating is not always reliable. Locking in a timeline would further bolster this important study, according to Luu Anh Tuyen of the Vietnam Atomic Energy Institute and Nguyen Quang Hung of Duy Tan University in Vietnam, who also conduct research at Óc Eo but were not involved with the new work. "The discovery of such global maritime trade routes will change the way our world views human history," they wrote in an e-mail to *Scientific American*, "and provide information on the missing chains on the world history's development."

Hsiao-chun Hung hopes the new study and her future work will help the world better understand Southeast Asia's place in history. "The role of Southeast Asia is often overlooked," she says. "This study highlights the importance of Southeast Asia in ancient times, as it served as a unique crossroads for migrants, merchants and travelers from different places."

About the Author

O. Rose Broderick is a freelance science journalist and former news intern at Scientific American *whose work focuses on energy, disability and disaster. Follow Broderick on Bluesky.*

Science Shows Why Traditional Kimchi Making Works So Well

By Rachel Crowell

Kimchi, an ancient staple of Korean cuisine, is traditionally fermented in handmade earthenware jars called *onggi*. But when it comes to mass production, companies use jars made of glass and other materials to ferment kimchi in large quantities. Now a new study demonstrates why some kimchi makers still swear by the traditional technology: *onggi* provide great environments for the growth of lactic acid bacteria, the "good" microbes that give kimchi its signature sour flavor.

"Having higher bacterial proliferation is nutritionally beneficial and generates [the] unique taste of fermented food," says Soohwan Kim, a mechanical engineering Ph.D. student specializing in fluid mechanics and biophysics at the Georgia Institute of Technology. For a study published last month in the *Journal of the Royal Society Interface*, Kim and his colleague compared an *onggi* with a glass jar and found the ceramic vessel produces kimchi with higher levels of lactic acid bacteria over the same fermentation time period. "There is a cultural belief that *onggi* used in fermented food makes the food better, but there isn't good science on it," Kim says. His work aims to change that.

Creating delicious kimchi is an artistic, scientific and culinary endeavor in which the fermentation process is key. Because many different factors affect that process, kimchi and other fermented foods are finicky, notes Maria L. Marco, a food microbiologist at the University of California, Davis. "Even within one particular food [made] using the same ingredients and same recipe, how can there be different flavors and outcomes to that fermentation? That's a big question we don't have all the answers to right now," says Marco, who wasn't involved with the new study.

In order to study the fermentation process, Kim and his doctoral adviser, Georgia Tech fluid dynamicist David Hu, used a combination of experimentation and mathematical modeling. They concluded that producing kimchi in an *onggi* enables more bacterial growth than doing so in a sealed glass jar. More importantly, the researchers uncovered what makes *onggi* ideal vessels for this process.

"I thought it was an interesting approach to try to begin to untangle how making fermented foods in different ways can affect the food that's made," Marco says.

The difference between the containers is related to their permeability, or how quickly liquid and gas can pass through them. Producing outstanding kimchi requires a Goldilocks situation, Kim says: fermentation vessels need to be semipermeable rather than overly permeable or impermeable.

Permeability is important because it influences the delicate dance between carbon dioxide and lactic acid bacteria. These microbes naturally migrate from soil to the vegetables growing in it, including the cabbage and other ingredients that form the base of kimchi. During the salty fermentation process, lactic acid and other types of bacteria flourish and expel carbon dioxide, which begins to build up in the container. The researchers' results demonstrate that the lactic acid bacteria "proliferate in a moderate carbon dioxide level," Kim says. But excessive carbon dioxide needs somewhere to go; otherwise it will grow to a high concentration that will eventually hinder the all-important bacterial growth. Conversely, if the container is too permeable, the carbon dioxide will escape too rapidly, reducing bacterial growth.

After Kim purchased an unglazed *onggi* from his hometown on Jeju Island, South Korea, he and Hu measured carbon dioxide levels as brined cabbage fermented in both the *onggi* and a tightly sealed glass jar. They carried out three trials per jar, sterilizing the containers in an autoclave before each trial. For accurate measurements, the researchers covered the *onggi* with a custom-made lid that could accommodate sensors for pressure, carbon dioxide and oxygen. They then used a thin plastic film to seal any remaining gaps between the sensors and the lid. Kim and Hu noted in the study that the glass jar leaked a little, albeit less than the *onggi*.

For two days per trial, the cabbage-filled *onggi* and glass jar rested in an oven set to 25 degrees Celsius. "I put that higher-than-usual [temperature] to accelerate the fermentation process," Kim says. While kimchi can be fermented at much lower temperatures, such as five degrees C, Kim notes that he and Hu assumed that the only change resulting from the higher temperature "is the speed of the process."

The researchers also used electron microscopy and computed tomography scans to probe the porous structure of the *onggi* and calculate its "gas permeability coefficient," or how easily gas could pass through it. They discovered that this value was more than double that of the glass jar. Because the *onggi* allowed carbon dioxide to escape more rapidly than its glass counterpart, lactic acid bacteria thrived. In the glass jar, where carbon dioxide wasn't released as quickly, the gas stifled bacterial growth. "The porous structure of the *onggi* mimics the loose soil where lactic acid bacteria [are] naturally found," the researchers wrote in their paper. This helps ensure that food fermented in the vessel teems with the microbes.

The researchers also demonstrated the *onggi*'s permeability with an experiment drawn from Korean culture: they filled the vessel halfway with saltwater and showed that within eight hours, salt deposits began coating its outer surface. "Korean culture calls it a 'salt flower,'" Kim says. This phenomenon is usually observed when Korean chefs ferment soy sauce (or *ganjang*) in *onggi*. When these salty blooms appear on the outside of an *onggi*, they are thought to signify that that particular vessel is permeable enough to produce top-notch sauces.

"Even in the ancient culture, [kimchi makers used] regulation of gas level to optimize the fermentation process," Kim says. Although large-scale kimchi producers combine glass, plastic or metal jars with a gas regulation system, Kim and Hu's work demonstrates that *onggi* can accomplish the same goal on their own.

Perhaps as a result of that ability, the traditional vessels are still in demand today: artisans continue to create *onggi* that kimchi enthusiasts can use to achieve quality fermentation.

About the Author

Rachel Crowell is a Midwest-based writer covering science and mathematics. Follow Crowell on Twitter @writesRCrowell

To Follow the Real Early Human Diet, Eat Everything

By Kate Wong

Paul Saladino is stripped to the waist, biceps bulging as he works a butcher's saw back and forth across a cow femur. When he finally severs the bone, a crowd of onlookers erupts in cheers. Flashing a smile, he checks to make sure he's being filmed, then scoops a spoonful of marrow from the center of one piece of bone. He then deposits it in the mouth of an eager young woman like a priest giving communion.

Saladino, a medical doctor, is a popular proponent of an animal-based diet that exalts meat and organs and demonizes vegetables. Through videos like this one on TikTok, as well as the podcast he hosts, he preaches the value of eating beef and liver, marrow and testicles to millions of followers on social media. He is the author of the 2020 book *The Carnivore Code* and a companion cookbook. He founded the company Heart and Soil, which sells organ-based supplements, and co-founded Lineage Provisions, which sells protein powder and meat sticks. Saladino contends that the traditional food pyramid, with its broad base of plant foods that narrows into animal foods, is upside down and that the medical establishment's view that high cholesterol causes heart disease is wrong. He says that meat and organs are the key to health, strength and vitality.

Saladino is not alone in his carnivorous pursuits. TikTok, Instagram and YouTube are teeming with influencers peddling meat-centric menus. Like the so-called paleo or caveman diets before them, these diets shun ultraprocessed foods such as potato chips, breakfast cereals, packaged breads, sodas and hot dogs. But they are significantly more restrictive than the paleo diet where plant foods are concerned. Some advocates, Saladino and celebrity adventurer Bear Grylls among them, allow for a limited amount of fruit but discourage vegetables, which they contend are loaded with defensive chemicals that are toxic to humans. Others, such as Canadian psychologist Jordan Peterson and his podcast host daughter, Mikhaila, champion a diet of beef, salt and water alone. Many, like social media personality Brian Johnson, aka Liver King, recommend consuming animal products–including dairy and eggs–raw.

Meatfluencers, as they are known, often characterize their regimens as "ancestral," made up of the foods our ancient predecessors ate. If this is what our ancestors ate, they argue, then this is what the human body is supposed to consume. "If you align your diet and lifestyle with millions of years of human and hominid evolution," Saladino says in another TikTok appearance, "that is how humans thrive."

Studies of the remains of our forebears, as well as observations of living primates and modern-day hunter-gatherers, refute the idea that humans evolved to subsist primarily on animals. Meat did play a significant role in our evolution. Yet that doesn't mean we're meant to eat like lions. Real ancestral human diets are difficult to reconstruct precisely, but they were vastly more varied than the mostly meat diets of carnivores, a finding that has important implications for what people today should eat to be healthy.

To be fair to the promoters of flesh-forward diets, scientists have traditionally paid a lot of attention to meat eating in human evolution, as have journalists who write about our origins (including me). Several factors have contributed to this trend. For one thing, we humans are unique among primates in regularly hunting animals that are as large as or larger than ourselves, and scientists are particularly interested in understanding traits that set us apart from other creatures. For another, stone tools and butchered animal bones are more readily preserved in the archaeological record than fragile plant remains. And then there's the fact that the hunting of animals–particularly large, dangerous mammals such as elephants–is inherently more exciting than the quiet business of gathering berries, nuts and tubers. In any case, it doesn't take a lot of googling to turn up a heap of scientific papers and popular articles touting the idea that hunting and eating meat made us human.

Interest in the role of meat and hunting in human origins has deep roots. Charles Darwin even speculated about its importance in his 1871 treatise, *The Descent of Man, and Selection in Relation to Sex*. Ideas about how carnivory shaped human evolution have shifted over the years, but the prevailing wisdom is this: around two million years ago *Homo erectus*, an early member of our genus, began evolving modern human body proportions, with longer legs, shorter arms, a smaller gut and a larger brain. The earliest stone tools and animal bones bearing cut marks date to before that period. The timing suggests that the invention of sharp-edged stone tools allowed early humans to butcher large animals and have access to a rich new source of calories. This nutritious food required less processing in the gastrointestinal tract, which allowed our energetically expensive gut tissue to shrink. Calorie-dense meat also provided fuel that allowed our energetically expensive brains to expand. A feedback loop took hold: as brains ballooned, our increasingly clever ancestors dreamed up ever more effective tools for procuring energy-rich animal foods, fueling more brain growth in *Homo*.

If that were all we knew about human evolution, it'd be tempting to conclude that we evolved to eat a meat-based diet. But that's only a piece of what anthropologists and archaeologists have learned about food and human origins, and even that chapter of our story has undergone revision over the past 15 years in light of new evidence. Fresh fossil discoveries and novel DNA analyses are revealing what our ancestors ate in unprecedented detail. For a clearer understanding of the evolution of humans and our diet, we need to take a closer look at what happened before and after that two-million-year mark.

Let's start at the beginning. Humans, monkeys and apes make up a subset of primates known as the higher primates, which evolved to eat fruit. The hominin lineage (*Homo sapiens* and its extinct relatives, including *Ardipithecus*, *Australopithecus*, and others) dates to roughly six million to seven million years ago. Fossils of the earliest known hominins indicate that they walked upright on two legs but still spent a lot of time in trees. They don't appear to have made stone tools and probably subsisted on a diet similar to that of chimpanzees and bonobos, our closest living relatives–which is to say mostly fruits, nuts, seeds, roots, flowers and leaves, along with insects and the occasional small mammal.

For the entire first half of our known history, hominins seem to have maintained this plant-based diet–they left no material trace of meat eating. It's not until nearly three million years after our lineage got its start that there's any evidence that they exploited large animals for food.

The oldest possible evidence of meat eating by hominins comes from Dikika, Ethiopia. There researchers found fragments of bone from goat- and cow-size mammals bearing marks suggestive of butchery that occurred at least 3.39 million years ago. The butcher, in this case, was probably *Australopithecus afarensis*, the small-brained, small-bodied hominin species to which the famous Lucy fossil belongs–the only hominin species known from this time and place. Although no tools were discovered, based on the pattern of damage to the bones, the researchers concluded that *A. afarensis* used sharp-edged stones to strip flesh from the bones and struck the bones with blunt stones to access the marrow inside.

The oldest stone tools come from the site of Lomekwi in northwest Kenya. Like the cut-marked bones from Dikika, these 3.3-million-year-old implements significantly predate the origin of our genus, *Homo*, and seem instead to be the handiwork of the small-brained australopiths. Both occurrences also appear to be isolated in time, a flash in the evolutionary pan, separated by the next oldest evidence for stone tools and butchery by hundreds of thousands of years.

It's only after two million years ago that hominins started to incorporate large game into their diet more routinely, according to Briana Pobiner, a paleoanthropologist at the Smithsonian National Museum of Natural History, who studies the evolution of meat eating in humans. The site of Kanjera South in southwestern Kenya, which records hominin activities from around two million years ago, is one of the earliest sites to preserve evidence of what researchers call persistent carnivory. There early members of *Homo* transported choice rocks from as many as 10 kilometers away to make their stone tools. They used these tools to extract meat and marrow from a variety of mammals that lived in the surrounding grasslands, from small antelopes to bovids the size of wildebeests. Some of the antelopes appear to have been acquired intact, presumably through hunting. The larger animals may have been scavenged. However they procured the carcasses, the Kanjera hominins butchered animals at this site repeatedly, over generations, the bones spanning a sediment layer three meters thick.

The hominins at Kanjera went back to this place again and again to butcher animals, but their pattern of persistent carnivory was not widespread elsewhere. Nor was it followed by a steady increase in meat eating over time, as would be expected in the feedback-loop scenario. W. Andrew Barr of George Washington University and his colleagues, including Pobiner, analyzed the evidence for hominin meat consumption in the zooarchaeological record of eastern Africa from between 2.6 million and 1.2 million years ago. Although the evidence for meat eating increases shortly after two million years ago with the debut of *H. erectus*, the first hominin to attain modern body proportions, the study found that this pattern is the result of a sampling bias: researchers have simply collected more archaeological material from this time period than from earlier intervals. Their findings, Barr, Pobiner and their co-authors concluded, did not support the hypothesis that meat made us human.

"When I think about changes in diet over time, I don't think the change was linear," Pobiner says. In many ways, the changes have been more about broadening the diet rather than progressing from vegetarian to meat eater, she explains. "Humans are omnivores," she says. "We've always been omnivores."

Even at Kanjera, with its impressive accumulation of butchered bones, meat wasn't the only food on offer. Analyses of the cutting edges of a sample of stone tools from the site revealed that most of the implements exhibit wear patterns characteristic of tools that have been used in experiments to chop herbaceous plants and their underground storage organs–those tubers, bulbs, roots and rhizomes that plants produce to store carbohydrates. A smaller proportion showed signs of animal-tissue processing.

As much as the evolution of meat eating is a focus of her work, Pobiner says, "that doesn't mean that I think that it was ever the most significant component of early human diets."

It's possible that early humans were targeting fat rather than meat when they first started butchering animals. Jessica Thompson of Yale University and her colleagues argue that before hominins invented stone tools suitable for hunting large animals, they may have used simpler implements to scavenge abandoned carcasses for their nutritious marrow and brains. Lean meat such as that from wild animals is energetically expensive to metabolize, and in the absence of fat in the diet, it can cause protein poisoning and other ills. Smashing scavenged bones to get to the marrow could have produced the extra nutrients needed to fuel brain growth before our ancestors developed the more complex technology needed for hunting.

The fat and meat of terrestrial mammals weren't the only possible source of extra calories for hungry hominins. Fish, shellfish, and other aquatic animals and plants sustained our forebears who lived near rivers, lakes and oceans. As early as 1.95 million years ago, *Homo* was exploiting fish and turtles, among other aquatic foods, in Kenya's Turkana Basin.

Our ancestors may have also wrung more calories from plant and animal foods by cooking them. Richard Wrangham of Harvard University has proposed that cooking, which makes food easier to chew and digest, may have provided *Homo* with the extra fuel needed to power a bigger brain. In 2022 researchers announced that they had found remains of fish that may have been cooked with controlled heat 780,000 years ago at the site of Gesher Benot Ya'aqov in Israel.

There is another place where scientists can look for clues to what early humans ate: their teeth. When researchers analyzed the tartar preserved in the stained teeth of two *Australopithecus sediba* individuals from South Africa, they found microscopic bits of silica from plants these hominins ate nearly two million years ago, including bark, leaves, sedges and grasses.

Even the Neandertals, our burly cousins who ruled Eurasia for hundreds of thousands of years and are known for having been skilled big-game hunters, consumed plants. Amanda Henry of Leiden University in the Netherlands and her colleagues found traces of legumes, dates and wild barley in the tartar on their fossilized teeth. And researchers led by Karen Hardy of the University of Glasgow discovered roasted starch granules in Neandertal teeth, indicating that they ate cooked vegetables. Some Neandertals might have even forgone animal flesh entirely: in a study co-led by Laura Weyrich of Pennsylvania State University, analyses of DNA preserved in the tartar of Neandertals found in El Sidrón cave in Spain turned up traces of pine nuts, moss and mushrooms–and no meat whatsoever.

Researchers have developed other techniques for studying what hominins put in their mouths and chewed, such as measuring the chemical isotopes in teeth, but these methods have important limitations: they can't determine the proportion of animal versus plant foods in the diet. To that end, another tartar study offers an inkling. James Fellows Yates of the Max Planck Institute for Evolutionary Anthropology in Leipzig, Germany, and his colleagues analyzed DNA from bacteria preserved in Neandertal tartar and compared it with bacterial DNA from the teeth of modern chimps, gorillas, howler monkeys and modern humans. The team found that the Neandertals and modern humans in its sample had a group of *Streptococcus* bacteria in their mouths that the nonhuman primates didn't have. These strep bacteria eat sugars from starchy foods, such as roots, seeds and tubers. Their presence in the mouths of the Neandertals and modern humans–but not the nonhuman primates, which eat mostly nonstarchy plant parts–indicates that *Homo* had adapted to eating an abundance of starchy plant foods by the time Neandertals and modern humans split from their last common ancestor around 600,000 years ago. This timing hints that a high-carb diet helped to power brain expansion in *Homo*.

Other features of teeth suggest additional leads in the quest to understand what our ancestors ate. If you look at hominin tooth morphology over time, says paleoanthropologist and evolutionary biologist Peter Ungar of the University of Arkansas, you see that australopiths had big, flat teeth with thick enamel—traits that indicate they were specialized for crushing hard foods such as seeds. *Homo*, for its part, evolved smaller teeth with crests that were better suited to eating tough foods, including meat. Yet we obviously lack the long, sharp canine teeth that carnivores have for stabbing and tearing at prey and the sharp-edged carnassial teeth for shearing flesh.

"We're not pure carnivores, we never were," Ungar says. "Our teeth are not designed for meat eating." That doesn't mean we can't survive on animal tissue, he notes—cutting and cooking both make meat easier for us to consume—but "anybody who's chewed on beef jerky long enough knows that our teeth really aren't designed for that. Or, for that matter, raw steak."

The microscopic pits and scratches that foods leave on the teeth reinforce this message. Whereas *Australopithecus* microwear patterns reflect a narrow range of food types, early *Homo* shows a somewhat wider range. Later members of our genus show microwear texture patterns that indicate they ate even more kinds of foods. Although these lines of evidence are limited, Ungar says, they suggest *Homo* became a more versatile eater, capable of consuming a wider variety of foods than its predecessors. This versatility would have served our ancestors well as they spread into new environments with a greater diversity of food types on offer.

Proponents of animal-based diets are fond of pointing to the Hadza, a group of foragers in northern Tanzania, to make their case for going hard on meat. Saladino and Liver King name-check them regularly in their social media videos. "I can tell you very clearly that the Hadza don't give a shit about vegetables. They don't really eat vegetables," says Saladino, who once visited the Hadza on an excursion set up for tourists.

Anthropologists who have lived with the Hadza and studied their diet for years would disagree. Herman Pontzer of Duke University notes that for decades researchers have observed that plant foods make up at least 50 percent of the Hadza diet. The Hadza are not unique in this regard. Hunter-gatherers around the world get roughly half their calories from plant foods and half from animal foods on average. But that average obscures the real value of the hunting-and-gathering strategy, which is that it allows people to subsist on a wide variety of diets depending on what's available in their environment at a given time of year. Long-term studies of the Hadza show that some months they may get most of their calories from honey; other months they may eat mostly plant foods, including root vegetables. There are times they hardly eat any meat at all.

What made humans so triumphant wasn't that we swapped out plants for animals but that we added hunting to our repertoire. Hunting and gathering reliably produces more calories a day than any other primate strategy, Pontzer says. The reason it works is that it's a mixed portfolio. "You have some people going after high-value, hard-to-get animals with a lot of protein and fat, which is great," he says. "And you have people who are going after more dependable plant foods. It's the balance of those things that makes it so successful."

Hunting and gathering produces so many calories, in fact, that people can afford to share them with other group members, including children, whose brains take longer to develop than in other species and who need more time to learn how to fend for themselves. A strict plant eater can't do that, because although the number of calories one can get every day eating plants is very dependable, it might not be high enough to produce a surfeit of calories. A strict meat eater, on the other hand, will have long periods of famine between feasts that do not, on average, generate extra calories. But when we put those two things together, Pontzer observes, we generate a surplus. And that surplus, he surmises, is the variable that's made energetically expensive human things such as large brains and extended childhood possible.

What the fossil, archaeological and ethnographic evidence indicates, then, is that there is no one diet that nature prescribed for us. What our ancestors ate varied dramatically over time and space, driven in no small part by what was available to them as seasons changed, climate shifted, and populations spread into new ecosystems. Forged in that crucible of uncertainty, we evolved the ability to survive and thrive on an impressive diversity of foods. Hunter-gatherers around the world eat diets with wildly different proportions of plant and animal foods, and all of them appear to be healthy, protected from heart disease, diabetes, and other maladies that are common in industrial populations.

So what is a person looking to eat healthily supposed to do? "I think what it says is you should feel liberated to try a bunch of different diets and find one that works for you," Pontzer says. But "when somebody tells you that there's only one way to eat, they are wrong, and you can stop listening."

About the Author

Kate Wong is an award-winning science writer and senior editor at Scientific American *focused on evolution, ecology, anthropology, archaeology, paleontology and animal behavior. She is fascinated by human origins, which she has covered for more than 25 years. Recently she has become obsessed with birds. Her reporting has taken her to caves in France and Croatia that Neandertals once called home, to the shores of Kenya's Lake Turkana in search of the oldest stone tools in the world, to Madagascar on an expedition to unearth ancient mammals and dinosaurs, to the icy waters of Antarctica, where humpback whales feast on krill, and on a "Big Day" race around the state of Connecticut to find as many bird species as possible in 24 hours. Kate is co-author, with Donald Johanson, of* Lucy's Legacy: The Quest for Human Origins. *She holds a bachelor of science degree in biological anthropology and zoology from the University of Michigan. Follow Wong on X (formerly Twitter) @katewong*

Gene Variant May Have Helped Ancient Humans Survive Starvation

By James Dinneen

About a million years ago a small mutation might have unlocked a big advantage for ancient humans. A recent study in *Science Advances* suggests that a variant of a critical stretch of DNA called the growth hormone receptor gene protected against starvation–in part by limiting individuals' body size during periods of resource scarcity. The variant was widespread among *Homo sapiens* and their relatives, although it suddenly plummeted in frequency beginning around 40,000 years ago, especially in East Asia and Eurasia. Many people still carry it today.

Previous research had linked the variant, called *GHRd3*, to characteristics such as smaller birth size and earlier sexual maturity, as well as other qualities that can benefit organisms when food is scarce, says the study's lead author Omer Gokcumen, an anthropologist at the University at Buffalo. Still, researchers wanted to know more precisely what role the mutation played in human evolution.

To dig deeper, Gokcumen and his colleagues turned to mice. Or rather they turned some mice into analogues of early humans. Using the genetic editing tool CRISPR-Cas9, the team deleted a section of mice's growth hormone receptor gene so it resembled the *GHRd3* variant. The modified mice were not especially different from ordinary ones when fed a regular diet. But when fed very little, the male carriers grew up to be smaller than their unmodified counterparts. Gokcumen's team also found that among a group of 176 modern human children who survived malnutrition, symptoms were less severe in boys and girls with *GHRd3*.

These findings could help explain why *GHRd3* has persisted for so long. Perhaps it paid to be small in times of scarcity, the researchers speculate–but in times of abundance large size won out. Changes in available resources could then have balanced the costs and benefits of different variants within a population. "It's a trade-off," Gokcumen says. "I would probably fare better than Arnold Schwarzenegger if we [each] had 1,000 calories a day."

The team's explanation is "plausible," says Megan Dennis, a geneticist at the University of California, Davis, who was not part of the study. She praises the functional experiments in mice but notes that the affected gene is involved in so many fundamental processes that it is difficult to pin down *GHRd3*'s most adaptive effects. "I was like, 'Wow, there's so much that could be happening here,'" Dennis says.

And the study researchers continue to wonder what could have caused this variant's decline around 40,000 years ago. Climate change, migration, and the advent of better hunting and fishing tools all could have had an impact. Or it could have been something else entirely, Gokcumen says: "That is a very strange time in human evolution."

About the Author

James Dinneen is a freelance journalist from Colorado based in Somerville, Mass.

Wine's True Origins Are Finally Revealed

By Mark Fischetti & Francesco Franchi

With just a sniff and a sip, trained sommeliers can often tell what region a wine came from: Douro in Portugal, Barossa in Australia, Napa or Sonoma in California. Experts in a specific locale can name the hillside—even how far up the hill—where a wine's grapes were grown because of the terroir, the combination of soil, topography and microclimate that imparts a characteristic taste. The geographic and genetic journeys that brought those grapes to those places, however, have been poorly understood.

A massive new study gives us the clearest picture yet of the prehistory of wine, overturning several commonly accepted narratives about when and where humans cultivated grapevines to make the world's wines. A large international group of researchers collected and analyzed 2,503 unique vines from domesticated table and wine grapes and 1,022 wild grapevines. By extracting DNA from the vines and determining the patterns of genetic variations among them, they found some surprises.

For centuries grape growers in different communities passed down lore about where their grapes came from. Some governments, particularly in Europe, designated appellations—strictly circumscribed regions with rules on how and where a wine such as burgundy, rioja or barolo was legally allowed to be produced. But genetic studies to discover where vines originated thousands of years ago began in earnest only 10 or 15 years ago.

One theme that emerged from these studies was that wild grapes grew in central Asia and dispersed westward as early humans migrated in that direction. But the genetic data in the huge study correct this story, says Wei Chen, a senior research scientist at Yunnan Agricultural University in China and one of the study's leaders. Genetic data indicate that 400,000 and 300,000 years ago grapes grew naturally across the western and central Eurasian continent. Roughly 200,000 years ago a cold, dry, ice-age climate slowly killed off vines in the central Mediterranean Sea region, cleaving vine habitat into two isolated areas: one to the west of the sea (today Portugal, Spain and France) and one to the east (roughly Israel, Syria, Turkey and Georgia). Around 56,000 years ago the eastern region separated again into smaller isolated areas: the Caucasus (Georgia, Armenia and Azerbaijan) and western Asia (Israel, Jordon and Iraq).

Until recently, researchers also thought humans domesticated grapevines from wild progenitors as long as 8,000 years ago as an early agricultural revolution spread across what is now western Asia and Europe. Some experts thought vines were first cultivated in Iberia (primarily Portugal and Spain) around 3,000 years ago. Other investigators thought domestication first happened in the Caucasus. To make matters murkier (not a good trait in wine), there was disagreement on whether grapes were used first for food ("table grapes") or for fermentation.

The recent study settles this debate: humans in western Asia domesticated table grapes around 11,000 years ago. Other people, in the Caucasus, domesticated wine grapes around the same time–although they probably didn't master winemaking for another 2,000 or 3,000 years.

Early farmers, the revised story goes, migrated from western Asia toward Iberia and brought table vines with them. Along the way the farmers crossbred the table vines with local wild grapevines. The earliest crossbreeding probably happened in what is now Israel and Turkey, creating muscat grapes, which are high in sugar–good for eating *and* fermenting. Gradually the table grape was genetically transformed into different wine grapes in the Balkans, Italy, France and Spain.

But if people in the Caucasus already had wine grapes, why didn't they bring them to Europe? "We just don't know yet," Chen says. People migrating from there–notably Yamnaya nomads 4,000 to 5,000 years ago–might have brought vines, but the genetic analysis shows that Caucasus grapes have had very little influence on the makeup of European wine grapes.

Once farmers did begin cultivating wine grapes in Europe, they developed many of the varietals we enjoy today. Some grapes, such as cabernet sauvignon, have the same name everywhere they are grown. Other varietals farmed in different regions took on different names even though the grapes are genetically identical, such as zinfandel and primitivo. Sadly, it is almost impossible to trace a current varietal back to western Asia or the Caucasus, the two early domestication centers. Over the centuries grape growers crossbred table and wine grapes, as well as domesticated and wild grapes, and even back bred offspring with parents. "Once they had a superior vine, they usually destroyed the prior vines," Chen says, making it hard to construct a family tree. You may never know where your favorite wine came from–really came from. In that sense, the mystique lives on.

About the Authors

Mark Fischetti has been a senior editor at Scientific American *for 17 years and has covered sustainability issues, including climate, weather, environment, energy, food, water, biodiversity, population, and more. He assigns and edits feature articles, commentaries and news by journalists and scientists and also writes in those formats. He edits History, the magazine's department looking at science advances throughout time. He was founding managing editor of two spinoff magazines:* Scientific American Mind *and* Scientific American Earth 3.0. *His 2001 freelance article for the magazine, "Drowning New Orleans," predicted the widespread disaster that a storm like Hurricane Katrina would impose on the city. His video* What Happens to Your Body after You Die?, *has more than 12 million views on YouTube. Fischetti has written freelance articles for the* New York Times, Sports Illustrated, Smithsonian, Technology Review, Fast Company, *and many others. He co-authored the book* Weaving the Web *with Tim Berners-Lee, inventor of the World Wide Web, which tells the real story of how the Web was created. He also co-authored* The New Killer Diseases *with microbiologist Elinor Levy. Fischetti is a former managing editor of* IEEE Spectrum Magazine *and of* Family Business Magazine. *He has a physics degree and has twice served as the Attaway Fellow in Civic Culture at Centenary College of Louisiana, which awarded him an honorary doctorate. In 2021 he received the American Geophysical Union's Robert C. Cowen Award for Sustained Achievement in Science Journalism, which celebrates a career of outstanding reporting on the Earth and space sciences. He has appeared on NBC's* Meet the Press, *CNN, the History Channel, NPR News and many news radio stations. Follow Fischetti on X (formerly Twitter) @markfischetti*

Francesco Franchi is an infographic designer and deputy creative director of la Repubblica.

Section 2: Cravings and Taste

We Are Living in a Golden Age of Apples

By Laura Helmuth

We are living in a golden age of apples, a time of delicious, diverse, mouth-watering abundance that we could barely have imagined at the turn of the millennium. How did we get to a time when most of us, most of the year, can eat our choice of fragrant, juicy, sweet, crisp (oh so crisp) apples?

We can thank a mix of science, innovations, investment in long-term research, the multi-multi-multi-generational transmission of knowledge, communal action and people who joyfully dedicate their lives to a cause.

What's *your* favorite apple? I asked this question on the social media platform Bluesky, and this is a sample of people's answers: Macoun, Winesap, Gravenstein, Winter Banana, CrimsonCrisp, SnapDragon, SweeTango, Jazz, Cosmic Crisp, Jonathan, Empire, Envy, RubyFrost, Hidden Rose, Sonata, Pink Lady, Regent, Honeycrisp, Honeycrisp, Honeycrisp. (My favorite? Evercrisp.)

Many of us remember that the U.S. apple market was dominated for decades by one variety: Red Delicious, which is a bold name for a bland apple. It is certainly red, with a lovely rich jewel color and a handsome shape. But *delicious*? The main alternative was Golden Delicious, a perfectly fine but similarly uninspiring yellow variety. Tart, green Granny Smiths, which were propagated in Australia in 1868 by an orchardist named Maria Ann Sherwood Smith, started taking a decent share of the market in the U.S. in the 1980s. And that's where we were stuck.

David Bedford, an apple researcher at the University of Minnesota who helps develop new varieties (his favorite apples: Honeycrisp, SweeTango and Rave) says, "I still remember some big marketers telling me: we have a red apple, a yellow apple, and a green apple. Do we really need any more?"

Apple History

Today's cultivated apples are produced by the tree *Malus domestica*. Its ancestor is *Malus sieversii*, which still grows wild in what is now Kazakhstan and bears small and variable fruit. Farmers began domesticating apples sometime between 10,000 and 4,000 years ago in the Tian Shan Mountains of Central Asia, according to genetic analyses. These cultivated varieties then quickly spread along the Silk Road trade route, where breeders crossed them with another wild species, *Malus sylvestris*. The ancient Romans developed techniques for apple grafting (more on that in a sec) and propagated the trees across their empire.

It's a little challenging to track the cultural history of apples because in many languages, the word that came to mean "apple" could refer to any type of fruit. There weren't apples in Mesopotamia, for instance, so the tempting fruit in the Garden of Eden story was more likely a fig. When the Greek goddess of discord inscribed a fruit with "For the most beautiful" and started the Trojan War, that fruit may have been a quince. And William Tell probably didn't shoot an arrow through an apple on top of his son's head. Isaac Newton wasn't hit on the head, but he did say that observing an apple falling from a tree helped inspire his theory of gravity.

Some legends are based in fact: Apples really were planted across the U.S. Midwest by John Chapman, an eccentric missionary nicknamed Johnny Appleseed. These apples were for juicing and fermenting into hard cider rather than eating. Some cider orchards went under during Prohibition, and many small-hold and backyard orchards were lost to disease or abandoned as people moved to cities. Industrial orchards specialized in a few varieties, and many specialty or rare varieties were no longer cultivated. A modern real-life legend named Tom Brown has rediscovered and saved about 1,200 historic apple varieties in Appalachia.

During the 20th century, people lucky enough to live near local orchards could eat distinctive regional apples. But these apples usually weren't produced in enough abundance to ship widely, and they were available only seasonally. (If you live within driving distance of Dickerson, Md., I highly recommend Kingsbury's Orchard, which has been in business since 1907 and is always experimenting with new varieties.) But for most of the world, most of the time, you had only a few mass-produced varieties to choose from. In the U.S. that meant red, yellow or green.

Before Honeycrisp and after Honeycrisp

Do you remember the first time you tasted a Honeycrisp apple? Bedford sure does. It was the 1980s, and he had recently started a job at the agricultural school of the University of Minnesota to work on fruit crops. "I can't remember all the things that swirled in my brain," Bedford says, "but one was the question 'What is this?'" The Honeycrisp he sampled as a test crop was so different from the Red Delicious apples he had grown up with, "and my knowledge was so limited that I was a little uncertain: 'Is this okay? Is this all right?'" But it didn't take him long to figure out that "not only is it all right but excellent."

Honeycrisp has a "disruptive trait," says Chris Gottschalk, a geneticist who works at the U.S. Department of Agriculture's research station in Kearneysville, W.V. (his favorite apples: Honeycrisp and Golden Russet). Honeycrisp's texture–the crispness–had never been combined with a high-acidity, high-sugar apple, he says. "That really struck North American consumers specifically well," Gottschalk says. As its popularity grew, it went from being largely a "u-pick" fruit to becoming regionally available in groceries, and now it is the third most produced apple in the U.S.

Bedford says the world of commercial apples has two phases: before Honeycrisp and after Honeycrisp. Before, there were basically two categories to describe texture, he says: soft/mealy or hard/firm/dense. "With Honeycrisp, we had to redefine what texture was," Bedford says. That texture was so distinctive and delightful that it has become the basis for many of our new apple varieties, which is why such a large number of them have the word "crisp" in their name. "Once you've had crisp," he says, "it's hard to go back."

Honeycrisp inspired consumer demand for excellent tasting apples, and that changed the apple market. "It wasn't that consumers wanted Red Delicious" back in the day, Bedford says. "They just didn't have any choice."

Paul Francis, an apple buyer for Giant grocery stores, says the company now carries more than 20 varieties throughout the year, twice the assortment it carried 10 years ago. He says, "The demand for premium variety apples has increased over the past few years dramatically." The grocery chain's most popular specialty varieties are Honeycrisp, Gala and Fuji. He and his produce team are particularly excited about some even newer varieties, including Hunnyz, SugarBee, Cosmic Crisp, Wild Twist and Evercrisp.

The most produced varieties across the U.S. in the 2023–2024 growing season, according to the U.S. Apple Association, a trade organization, are Gala, Red Delicious, Honeycrisp, "others" (including all the new and specialty varieties that don't yet rank individually) and Fuji. Cosmic Crisp is climbing up the charts while Red Delicious is plummeting as a proportion of all apples produced.

How to Breed a Better Apple

One common misconception about apples is that they "breed true," says Susan Brown, an apple researcher at Cornell University's College of Agriculture and Life Sciences. They don't: if you plant a Gala seed, you won't grow a tree that produces Gala apples. (Brown's favorite apple: "SnapDragon, without a doubt," she says. Her team cultivated SnapDragons and they were served at her daughter's wedding.) Apples don't self-fertilize; one tree's flowers need pollen from a different tree. That means any seed from a Gala apple is 50 percent Gala and 50 percent "whatever the bee brought," Brown says. Even the seeds within a given apple can have different genetic compositions. So when you're developing new varieties, she says "you play the genetic lottery every time."

Breeders start with a parent tree and cross it with another variety that they think will make a favorable combination of traits. (When one parent is a Honeycrisp, the offspring typically inherit the "Crisp" name.) At the USDA, Gottschalk and his colleagues use a glass rod to painstakingly rub pollen from the other parent's stamen onto the flowers' style and stigma to control fertilization. Other breeders may throw a net over a blossoming tree, stick a bouquet of flowering boughs from another tree inside the net, put some bees in and, Gottschalk says, "let the bees do the work for you."

Once the blossoms are fertilized, the parent tree produces apples, and their seeds are harvested, chilled for a season and sprouted. After a few months, when the new crosses are at the seedling stage, they can be tested for the presence or absence of certain genes.

The apple genome is enormous, complex and highly variable, and even with controlled fertilization, you don't know which versions of a gene (called alleles) from the parent trees made it through to the seedlings. Most interesting qualities are influenced by many genes. Brown says one of the surprises over the course of her career studying apple genetics has been "the complexity of traits we thought would be easy." There's always another gene or transcription factor involved.

But there are a few genetic markers that breeders can screen for at the seedling stage, Gottschalk says, that give a good indication of acidity, skin color, resistance to certain diseases or the "crisp" trait in Honeycrisp and its progeny. The seedlings with the right constellation of traits are allowed to develop and go through the grafting process.

Grafting is the only way to "fix the genetics," Brown says. New seedlings or branches that produce the desired fruit are notched into a "rootstock" apple tree. The rootstock provides structure and nutrition for its newly grafted branches, but it does not determine the shape, flavor or other qualities of the apples produced by the grafts, which are essentially all clones. (Fertilization doesn't make a difference for how an apple turns out, either; whatever the bees bring in determines only the genes in its seeds.)

One of the great advances in apple breeding in the past few decades has been the widespread use of dwarf rootstocks. These trees mature quickly at a smaller size than traditional apple trees but can still support a lot of grafts. A greater proportion of energy can then go into growing apples rather than developing thick, tall, gnarly trees. Breeders can plant the trees closer together to make test plots more efficient, and boughs grafted to a dwarf rootstock start producing apples two to three years earlier than those grafted to a traditional rootstock.

And that's when the fun begins because a big part of an apple breeder's job is tasting apples. "We have many sophisticated tests to measure firmness, texture, Brix [the amount of dissolved sugar] or acidity," Brown says, "but there is no substitute for biting and eating the apple, so that is a large part of the process. Yes, we get upset stomachs, but one good apple makes up for it."

"At the peak of crunch times, I've had to taste 600 apples a day," Bedford says. "The first 100 are okay, but after that, it gets to be real work."

No robot or genetic test can determine whether a new hybrid apple is good or not. People decide whether an apple is worth cultivating. And most of them are not. "Even with careful breeding and DNA analysis, only a small percentage are good enough" Bedford says. "In the best case, we get some combination of genes we didn't fully see in either parent, and that's exactly what Honeycrisp was."

Apple breeders continue to test new varieties for five to 15 years after the initial taste test to screen for disease resistance, heat resilience, winter hardiness, the ability to bear every year (some bear only every other year) and other traits. "They all have bad traits; there's no perfect apple," Bedford says. He estimates that only one out of 10,000 seedlings he and his colleagues develop are good enough to release commercially.

What's Next for Apples

I spoke with several apple researchers while working on this story, and do you know who loves their jobs? Apple researchers. And that's not just because they get to taste new varieties all the time and spend workdays in an orchard. All of them, as well as the other orchardists and hobbyists I know, are proud of the progress they've made in the past few decades and optimistic about the future.

One of the biggest challenges to developing new varieties is that the ones we have now are *so good*. "The bar has risen so much," Bedford says. Any new apple variety must be better than what already exists to justify developing it and bringing it to market. "We are some of our biggest competition," he says. But every year a few of those 600 apples a day he bites into have a different combination of qualities that make them worth developing, something never tasted before.

Apple researchers are busy. Brown, Bedford and Gottschalk spend about as much time in the lab as they do in their test orchards. They're looking for more genes associated with favorable (or unfavorable) traits. They're working on apples that are well suited to selling as slices. They're making crosses that have the right qualities for hard cider. And some breeders are developing new varieties of small apples that a child can easily hold and eat. Isn't that adorable?

The technology for storing apples is improving quickly, and new varieties are being bred to stay firm for longer. Packing houses are experimenting with ways to control temperature, balance oxygen and carbon dioxide levels and scrub out ethylene gas that promotes ripening and rotting. Brown once tasted an apple that had been stored for three years, and she says she never would have guessed it was that old. Researchers are hoping to make apples last a full year in storage, expanding when and where they can be sold. (Some apple varieties available now can last for months in a home refrigerator, so stock up on Pink Ladies and Evercrisps when the apple season starts to wind down.)

A lot of apple advancements have been made possible by long-term investment in research at the USDA and universities, as well as collaborations and communication among labs and growers and buyers. Gottschalk's team at the USDA, for instance, specializes in creating parent trees with lots of favorable traits that breeders at universities or commercial growers can use to cross with other parents and experiment with new varieties. Apples aren't a hugely profitable industry, and it takes a long time to determine whether a new variety will be a success, so funding this sort of research makes it all possible.

"The work that my predecessors and academics have done has laid the groundwork to rapidly accelerate innovation in apples," Gottschalk says. "In the next 15 to 20 years, we're going to see apples that address consumer traits, have fruits that are more resilient to disease and stress and are more efficient and sustainable and profitable." And they will be even more delicious (truly delicious, not Red Delicious).

What a great time to be alive. What a great time to be snacking. Isn't it a joy to hold a pinnacle of human achievement in your hand ... and take a bite?

About the Author

Laura Helmuth was formerly editor in chief of Scientific American. *She previously worked as an editor for the* Washington Post, National Geographic, Slate, Smithsonian *and* Science. *She is a former president of the National Association of Science Writers. She is currently a member of the National Academies of Sciences, Engineering, and Medicine's standing committee on advancing science communication and an advisory board member for SciLine and The Transmitter. She has a Ph.D. in cognitive neuroscience from the University of California, Berkeley. She recently won a Friend of Darwin Award from the National Center for Science Education. Follow her on Bluesky @laurahelmuth.bsky.social*

The Science of Melting Cheese

By Meghan Bartels

From pizza to panini and from quiche to quesadilla, melted cheese plays a starring role in countless culinary classics. But why do some cheeses melt into ooey-gooey deliciousness, and others simply don't? Forget black holes or the origins of life–this is the sort of question that science was created to address.

"Cheese melting is a very complex phenomenon," says Prateek Sharma, a food scientist at Utah State University. "When people eat cheese, they should think about what may be going on inside the cheese at the molecular level."

At that level, the process by which all the action happens involves a protein called casein. In milk, casein delivers the vital nutrients calcium and phosphate to a calf, lamb or baby. But the cheese-making process turns casein into a network held together by weak bonds and studded with molecules of water and fat.

In general, the dissolution of that network–the melting of the cheese–plays out in stages as the cheese is heated, Sharma says. First, beginning as cool as around room temperature, the cheese's assorted fats will begin to melt and seep out of the network, floating to the surface (this is why cheese gets sweaty). Next, as the cheese reaches the temperature of water from a hot tap, the proteins within it start losing water, shrinking and softening. By around 160 degrees Fahrenheit, about the temperature of thoroughly cooked meat, the melting process is complete, Sharma says. "Everything is molten," he adds.

But thoroughly melted cheese doesn't act like typical melted substances. When ice, butter and chocolate melt, they become liquid: they flow and drip. In contrast, mozzarella oozes and stretches, making it the poster cheese for good melting.

The magic happens thanks to casein–more specifically, as a function of the loose interactions between casein molecules. The casein network needs to be flexible enough to move but rigid enough that the cheese hangs together. Increasing the amount of water or fat locked into the casein network can encourage melting, but so can modifying the casein itself.

For a satisfying melt, cheese needs a Goldilocks level of bonds between molecules of calcium phosphate embedded in the casein that lock together the protein network. "If you have too much calcium content, cheese will not melt," Sharma says. "If there is too little calcium, then it will melt very fast, so it will be runny."

Cheese makers' key tool in adjusting the number of these bonds is acidity, says John Lucey, a food scientist at the University of Wisconsin–Madison and director of the Wisconsin Center for Dairy Research. In cheese made at a relatively neutral pH, there are enough calcium bonds that casein molecules are stiffly bound to each other.

Add some acid, and things start to loosen up in the resulting cheese. "That dissolves some of the calcium and phosphate bonds—just enough of them that the system becomes more fluid," Lucey says. But add too much acid, and so many calcium bonds dissolve that charged areas on casein molecules can attract each other directly and continue to interact tightly enough to prevent stretch in the finished cheese. A good melt requires just the right amount of acid.

A second phenomenon affecting the way a cheese melts is the aging process. As cheese matures, enzymes and microorganisms inside of it can snip the casein molecules themselves. With more of this snipping, the cheese melts more easily but is less able to stretch and more likely to become soupy.

All this emphasis on the role casein plays in how cheese melts also helps to explain why vegan cheese—with no casein at all—is relatively soft even when chilled and often downright unappetizing when heated. "Plant-based cheeses, they start off as cold Jell-O, and then they become hot Jell-O," says Neil Cunningham, a materials scientist at the Center for Industrial Rheology in England, who has compared these cheeses with dairy ones.

Ricotta is another poor melter, even though it isn't vegan. That's because it's made from whey, the liquid left over from making cheeses. This starting material means that ricotta contains a little casein but mostly consists of whey proteins that build a very different type of structure—one that is characterized particularly by permanent bonds between sulfur molecules, Sharma says. Those permanent bonds make it much harder to truly melt ricotta; it merely softens.

But when casein dominates, understanding how acid and aging have affected the protein structure goes a long way in explaining the different melting characteristics of different cheeses. Compared with mozzarella, "something like feta is much more brittle and chalky and crumbly," Lucey says. That's because of the high acid content. On the other end of the spectrum, panela won't melt—there's not enough acid. "It's just held together too robustly—it's not fluid," Lucey says. A blue cheese may start out quite acidic and hard to melt but become less so as it ages and microbes break down the acids. "Eventually," he says, "you might be able to melt some of that into a kind of liquid pool." Lower moisture levels make Parmesan less conducive to melting.

For Lucey, this is the marvel of cheese-making: most varieties are the same milk treated in slightly different ways, all built on centuries of experimentation. "That's why you get hundreds of different types of cheese," he says. "It gives you artistic license to change anything that you want to and see how it turns out."

About the Author

Meghan Bartels is a science journalist based in New York City. She joined Scientific American *in 2023 and is now a senior news reporter there. Previously, she spent more than four years as a writer and editor at Space.com, as well as nearly a year as a science reporter at* Newsweek, *where she focused on space and Earth science. Her writing has also appeared in* Audubon, Nautilus, Astronomy *and* Smithsonian, *among other publications. She attended Georgetown University and earned a master's degree in journalism at New York University's Science, Health and Environmental Reporting Program.*

Period Food Cravings Are Real. A New Brain Finding Could Explain Why They Happen

By Jocelyn Solis-Moreira

The insatiable hunger that often accompanies a period is a very real feeling, but that increased craving for carbs and sweets has not been fully understood by science. Now new research suggests a possible mechanism in the brain that could help explain food cravings related to the menstrual cycle.

A small clinical trial published Thursday in *Nature Metabolism* has uncovered differences in insulin sensitivity at different phases of the menstrual cycle. While food cravings were not directly studied in the research, the authors suggest that an increased sensitivity to insulin—a hormone that regulates glucose levels, metabolism and food intake—could explain the jump in appetite.

"The brain contributes to metabolic changes and probably changes eating behavior across the menstrual cycle," says Martin Heni, a professor of endocrinology at Ulm University Hospital in Germany and co-senior author of the study. "This is nothing bad. It's physiological, but it may explain what many women report to us about what they feel across the menstrual cycle. This can be one underlying mechanism."

Insulin is produced in the pancreas, but it can cross the blood-brain barrier and can then target cells in several brain areas to regulate bodily processes. Previous research from Heni's team found that insulin in the brain can help suppress glucose production and stimulate glucose uptake in muscle tissue—indicators of its important role in managing metabolism and energy for the entire body. This relationship between the brain's insulin and body metabolism was only tested in young men, however.

The fact that sex hormones fluctuate across the menstrual cycle has held back research on insulin changes in people who menstruate. But bodily processes such as the uterus' preparation for potential pregnancy could cause differences in how the brain governs glucose metabolism. In one of two experiments, Heni's team recruited 11 women who reported that they have regular menstrual cycles. The researchers studied the changes that took place when the participants underwent two phases of the menstrual cycle: the follicular phase and the luteal phase. The follicular phase is when an egg is being prepared for ovulation, which usually begins on the first day of a period and ends once ovulation happens. The luteal phase starts after ovulation and is when the egg travels to the uterus, where it waits to potentially be fertilized. The team's study approach "turned out to be a good idea, because we saw big differences between the two cycle phases," Heni says.

The researchers attached insulin clamps–considered the gold standard for measuring sensitivity to the hormone–to each of the 11 women, who had a median age of 24. The clamps measured sensitivity after researchers delivered either insulin or a placebo through a nasal spray in each session in addition to giving participants intravenous insulin. This technique helped quickly supply a large amount of insulin directly to the brain. Each participant underwent four sessions: two were conducted in their cycle's follicular phase, and the other two occurred in the luteal phase.

During the participants' follicular phase, when a period typically begins, the brain was more sensitive to the effects of insulin. This sensitivity disappeared once women entered the luteal phase, suggesting a switch to insulin resistance.

The new findings suggest that insulin resistance in the brain could make it more difficult to regulate energy production for the rest of the body. It's also possible that the resistance could interfere with insulin's other roles, such as controlling appetite. Studies of conditions such as obesity and diabetes have linked increased insulin and heightened insulin sensitivity with the sensation of satiety, or reduced appetite. Insulin resistance, on the other hand, is thought to increase food cravings. Although the team did not formally test subjects' food intake in the current study, Heni says the findings could help explain why people experience food cravings in the second half of the menstrual cycle. If so, this would align with research reporting an increase in food cravings during the luteal phase.

To confirm their findings, the researchers conducted a second experiment using neuroimaging to get a closer look at brain activity across the menstrual cycle. They worked with a separate group of 15 women with a median age of 23. The imaging revealed a similar pattern of insulin sensitivity, specifically in the hypothalamus, a brain area that acts as a control center for food intake and metabolism.

One of the limitations to the study was its small sample size, which can skew the results of any trial. Maintaining large participant numbers for experimental, observational studies such as these is a challenge, however–particularly because these studies require participants to go through the experiments multiple times, says Alexandra DiFeliceantonio, a Virginia Tech neuroscientist who studies how the brain modulates food preference and who was not involved in the new research. "You will always end up with less participants because it's expensive and time consuming," she says.

Still, the changes in brain insulin sensitivity recorded within each participant were "striking," says Nils Kroemer, a neuroscientist at the University of Bonn in Germany, who was not involved in the research but wrote an accompanying Nature editorial on the study. The results, he says, support a need for a larger-scale study in the future. A larger trial could also consider other factors that may affect energy metabolism, including obesity, birth control use or underlying endocrine diseases, such as polycystic ovary syndrome, that are linked to insulin resistance.

The current findings could suggest a neural mechanism that might explain period cravings, Kroemer suggests. He proposes that hypothalamic circuits involved in energy metabolism could also be intertwined with those coordinating motivation–including the ones involved in food-seeking behavior. "It may explain some changes [in the menstrual cycle] that have been very difficult to pinpoint to a particular mechanism," Kroemer says.

The hypothalamic circuit could also possibly tie into what is already known about how the brain promotes food cravings, which DiFeliceantonio says has largely to do with the release of the hormone dopamine. The brain chemical is responsible for making a person feel and seek pleasurable experiences, such as indulging in a favorite snack. But DiFeliceantonio says that it's likely that additional variables and processes in the body, such as those that happen in the menstrual cycle, can influence food cravings as well. Further research is needed to better understand the mechanisms that stimulate hunger and food cravings during periods.

About the Author

Jocelyn Solis-Moreira is a freelance journalist covering health and science. She is based in New York State.

Food Can Be Literally Addictive, New Evidence Suggests

By Marta Zaraska

Given the option, most rats will choose sugar instead of cocaine. Their lust for the carbohydrate is so intense that they will go as far as to self-administer electric shocks in their desperation to consume sugar. Rats aren't alone in this drive. Humans, it seems, do something similar. People who've had bariatric surgery sometimes continue to overindulge in highly processed foods, those made from white flour, sugar, butter, and the like, even if it means later enduring vomiting and diarrhea. Daily snacking on processed foods, recent studies show, rewires the brain's reward circuits. Cravings for tasty meals light up the brain just like cravings for cocaine do, prompting some researchers to ask whether products such as fries or cookies can trigger addiction akin to that associated with drugs or alcohol.

Yet the issue is by no means settled. An ongoing debate persists over whether these foods are truly addictive. Processed foods might provoke compulsive behaviors that reinforce the need to consume more, but do they really have mood-altering effects, another criterion used to define an addiction?

Answers to these questions are complicated by the enormous variety of foods we consume. There is no single opiatelike substance that can be identified as leading someone to become a food addict. Arguments in favor of food addiction suggest that if carbohydrates and fats are mixed together in unnaturally large doses, this creates a rapid "delivery system" for nutrients that results in physiological effects on the brain's reward system that resemble those produced by cocaine or nicotine.

To examine how this affects actual behaviors, researchers developed a measurement to examine the strong pull that highly processed food exerts on humans. In 2009 the Yale Food Addiction Scale emerged. It is used to assess whether a person displays behavioral patterns that would merit fries, shakes and other palatable foods being classified as addictive substances.

Using this measurement technique, a 2022 meta-analysis suggested that 20 percent of adults are addicted to food. People in this group go out of their way to obtain their favorite foods and often eat to the point of feeling physically ill. They experience withdrawal, fail to quit eating certain foods and continue their consumption pattern despite adverse consequences, such as disruptions to their daily routines and social activities. These are all criteria set out by the Yale Food Addiction Scale, which is adapted from measures used to gauge substance use disorders. The definition of food addiction is separable from obesity. Surprisingly, many people who tick the boxes for food addiction maintain a typical weight. If anything, food addiction is the closest cousin to binge eating disorder, says Alexandra DiFeliceantonio, a neuroscientist at the Fralin Biomedical Research Institute at Virginia Tech Carilion. Both cause people to exhibit a lack of control in the way food is consumed, but the definition for a substance use disorder also includes cravings, withdrawal symptoms and continued use despite negative consequences.

Critics of this research suggest that you can't get addicted to something that's essential to life. What's more, while science has pinpointed nicotine in cigarettes and ethanol in wine or beer as the substances responsible for keeping people hooked, no such clear-cut equivalent exists for food. "It's very difficult to prove that there are these nutrients in food that directly cause addiction," says Johannes Hebebrand, a psychiatrist at the University of Duisburg-Essen in Germany.

Yet Ashley Gearhardt, a clinical psychologist at the University of Michigan, argues that highly processed foods are vastly different from what our ancestors used to consume. "Foods that are very high in fat and carbohydrate in a kind of an equal ratio–they don't exist naturally," she says. "It's something that's designed by food scientists in a laboratory to look a certain way, feel a certain way in your mouth, smell a certain way when you open the package."

A 2021 study showed, for example, that people with binge eating disorder exclusively overeat ultraprocessed foods. "People aren't losing control over beans," Gearhardt says.

Early research on rats suggested that sucrose keeps animals hooked. "They want more and more and more. Each day, they'll show signs of craving," says Nicole Avena, a neuroscientist at the Icahn School of Medicine at Mount Sinai. Sugars are present in many natural foods, from bananas to beets. Yet, as Avena points out, it's all about packaging. A piece of fruit, she says, "has the appropriate amount of sugar in it, based on how much fiber it contains. Also, it has other nutrients that are going to minimize or mitigate the effects that that sugar might have on our brain."

What matters, the scientists argue, is the dosage and the speed of absorption of a substance. Most people don't consume pure ethanol, for example. Instead they opt for wine or beer, which contain a small amount of the addictive substance. (Most beer is more than 90 percent water.) Similarly, few of us indulge in sucrose by the spoonful. Nicotine also mixes with other ingredients and is carefully dosed. It's naturally present in eggplants and tomatoes, but you won't become an addict by indulging in vegetables.

When it comes to ultraprocessed snacks, sugar often goes together with fat–a combination that could make such foods even more addictive. A 2018 study by DiFeliceantonio and her colleagues showed that, compared with equally caloric foods containing only fat or only a carbohydrate, those made with both ingredients are far more efficient at activating the striatum, a part of the brain's reward center that is implicated in addictions.

For a 2023 study, DiFeliceantonio and her colleagues randomly assigned 82 people to snack on either high-fat, high-sugar yogurts or low-sugar, low-fat ones for eight weeks. The scientists discovered not only that the first group's preference for the healthier yogurts decreased after the trial but that their brain activation patterns changed, too. When they tasted fatty, sugary milkshakes, those who had been indulging in high-fat, high sugar snacks had an increased response in their reward circuits, including the striatum.

"Ultraprocessed foods are hijacking the brain in a way you'd see with addiction to drugs," Avena says.

One of the hallmarks of drug addiction, she says, is the release of dopamine in the brain's reward regions. The potency of a fatty, sugary treat in triggering this release was highlighted by a 2023 study in which scientists used positron-emission tomography on a small sample of volunteers. The results showed that indulging in a milkshake leads to a significant release of dopamine in healthy people that can be about one third of what is usually seen with amphetamines–a group of highly addictive stimulant drugs, such as "speed."

The addictive potential of ultraprocessed foods may not relate just to dopamine, however. A 2023 study revealed the importance of the cannabinoid receptor 2 (CB2) in getting hooked on certain foods (in this particular case, chocolate-flavored pellets, because the subjects were mice). Rodents lacking these receptors in the brain are not only less likely to become addicted to cocaine or alcohol, the research showed, but also less prone to food addiction–a finding that may open new paths for treatment of binge eating.

Research on weight-loss drugs provides further evidence that overeating and substance misuse may share common brain processes. Semaglutide (sold under the brand names Ozempic and Wegovy) induces weight loss by mimicking the insulin-increasing gut hormone glucagonlike peptide-1 (GLP-1), and it could potentially aid those struggling with various addictions, too. Animal experiments suggest, for example, that it can reduce dependence on cocaine and opioids. "That supports the argument that foods and drugs, in many ways, can act on the same brain systems," Avena says.

What's more, both illegal drugs and processed foods can induce cravings in the same reward areas of the brain–as demonstrated by a 2023 functional magnetic resonance imaging (fMRI) study. When researchers showed pictures of cocaine to drug addicts or photographs of donuts to healthy people, the same brain regions–ranging from the ventral striatum and amygdala to the cerebellum–lit up in both groups. And the stronger the volunteers' reported craving was, the more intense their neural response was as well.

Withdrawal symptoms, another classic feature of addiction, also seem to be present in connection with ultraprocessed foods. While it's unlikely that anyone experiences physical shakes from quitting cookies, parents who attempt to restrict their children's intake of sugar-sweetened drinks have reported symptoms such as headaches, irritability and social withdrawal in their kids. Similarly, adolescents instructed to abstain from their high intake of sodas for three days complained of decreased motivation and ability to concentrate–along with increased headaches.

Critics of the idea that certain foods may be addictive point out that treats such as burgers don't induce the same kind of "high" that one might experience with opioids or alcohol. "This is totally missing in all the food addiction stories," Hebebrand says. For her part, Gearhardt is not convinced. "By that principle, cigarettes are not addictive, right? You can drive your car while you smoke cigarettes. You can watch your children while you smoke cigarettes," she says. She points to studies indicating that chocolate does have a psychoactive effect and can induce feelings of euphoria at least as much as intravenous nicotine given to smokers can.

In 2022 Gearhardt and DiFeliceantonio published an opinion piece in the journal *Addiction* arguing that highly processed foods should be classified as addictive based on a 1988 Surgeon General report on tobacco products. That document outlined scientific evidence behind cigarettes' addictive nature, including their psychoactive effects and potential to trigger compulsive use. Similar evidence, the scientists argue, already exists for ultraprocessed foods. "If we apply that same criteria to this specific class of foods, it meets every single checkbox," Gearhardt says.

Hebebrand worries, however, that rushing to classify certain foods as addictive could let the sugar industry off the hook too easily. "They can always say, 'Well, this is a matter of debate; we don't know if it really exists,'" he says. The industry has already sponsored research that argues against the existence of sugar addiction, which, for Gearhardt, suggests that it may be following "the playbook of the tobacco industry." After all, nicotine wasn't a clear-cut candidate for an addictive substance, either: it lacks significant mind-altering effects and is not found in large amounts in foods, and researchers don't know the dosage at which it becomes addictive. As a result, and with the help of the tobacco industry, the addictive nature of tobacco was denied for decades. Considering ultraprocessed foods' detrimental health effects–a 2021 meta-analysis showed such products raise mortality risk by 25 percent–Gearhardt argues that it's better to chance misclassifying ultraprocessed foods as addictive than to fail to label them as such when warranted. "It's cigarettes all over again," she says.

About the Author

Marta Zaraska is a freelance writer based in France and author of Growing Young: How Friendship, Optimism and Kindness Can Help You Live to 100 *(Appetite by Random House, 2020). She wrote "Shrinking Animals" in the June 2018 issue of* Scientific American.

Your Genes May Influence What You Like to Eat

By Lauren J. Young

You are what you eat–and what you eat may be encoded in your DNA. Studies have indicated that your genetics play a role in determining the foods you find delicious or disgusting. But exactly how big a role they play has been difficult to pin down. "Everything has a genetic component, even if it's small," says Joanne Cole, a geneticist and an assistant professor at the University of Colorado School of Medicine. "We know that there is some genetic contribution to why we eat the foods we eat. Can we take the next step and actually pinpoint the regions in the genome?"

New research led by Cole has gotten a step closer. Through a large-scale genomics analysis, her team has identified 481 genome regions, or loci, that were directly linked to dietary patterns and food preferences. The findings, which have not yet been peer-reviewed, were presented last month at the American Society for Nutrition's annual flagship conference. They build on a 2020 *Nature Communications* study by Cole and her colleagues that used data from the U.K. Biobank, a public database of the genetic and health information of 500,000 participants. By scanning genomes, the new analysis was able to home in on 194 regions associated with dietary patterns and 287 linked to specific foods such as fruit, cheese, fish, tea and alcohol. Further understanding how genetics impact how we eat could reveal differences in nutritional needs or disease risks.

"One of the problems with a lot of these genomics studies is that they're very small. They don't have enough people to really be able to identify genes in ways that are credible. This study had a huge cohort of people, so that's really powerful," says Monica Dus, an associate professor at the University of Michigan, who wasn't a part of the new research but studies the relationship between genes and nutrition. "The other thing that I thought was really great is that they have so many different traits that they're measuring in respect to diet. They had cholesterol, the body, socioeconomic backgrounds."

As the research advances, Dus says such genome analyses could possibly help health care providers–and even policymakers–address larger issues that affect food access and health. "Instead of trying to obsess over telling people to eat this or that, a more powerful intervention is to link it to making sure there aren't 'food deserts' or to make sure that there's a higher minimum wage–things that have a broader impact," she says.

Scientific American spoke with Cole about the new research and what it tells us about the relationship between our genetics and food.

[An edited transcript of the interview follows.]

Q: What do we know about the link between genetics and diet?

A: There has been research on it for more than 100 years. Some of the earliest studies are heritability studies. Heritability is the amount of genetics that contribute to a trait. So traits such as height, which is very genetic, can have a 50 to 80 percent heritability. But diet probably has a really small heritability, or genetic component, because it's influenced by so many other important things such as socioeconomic status, culture, upbringing and all these other factors that have nothing to do with how you taste or like foods. It wasn't until newer methods came out in the past 15 years or so that we could use thousands of distantly related individuals [to study genetic associations with foods]. It helped remove that messy environmental component, and we could get more accurate estimates of heritability.

In 2020 I did a heritability analysis where we scanned the genome to find regions that were statistically associated [with foods and diet] and narrowed those regions down. I found that the median of the genetic component of most dietary traits was only about 5 percent. So it meant that they are super environmental traits–*but* it doesn't mean that that 5 percent is nothing. Because we have those big data now, we can study that 5 percent.

Q: What did you find in your recent genome association analyses?

A: We found regions in the genome that are likely influencing a variety of dietary traits, including things like fruit, poultry or fish intake or different kinds of coffee or alcohol intake. We were also able to see some genetic associations with more complicated dietary patterns, such as if you eat a healthy versus unhealthy diet.

Some of the genes that had the strongest effect on diet, which I find most compelling, are the taste receptor, olfactory receptor and digestive enzyme genes. This includes the bitter taste receptor gene—most prominently known for influencing intake of cruciferous vegetables, such as Brussels sprouts. In most of our diets, we eat various foods together, so the foods we eat are often connected to each other. But the olfactory receptor genes we identified were so specific. One was associated with cheese and nothing else. There's one very specific to fruit. There's one very specific to vegetables. There's one very specific to coffee.

There was one region in the genome for an olfactory receptor associated with how much tea someone drinks—that has a really fascinating story. Researchers have found a genotype, or a different version of a genetic variant, that explains someone's ability to smell a compound called beta-ionone. If you have one version of this olfactory receptor gene, then you can smell beta-ionone, and if you have the other version, you [are less sensitive to the smell or] can't smell it at all. It actually turns out that beta-ionone is in a bunch of things—such as tobacco, grapes, orange juice, papaya, peaches, raspberries, spearmint and tea. So this one version of this genotype may dictate—a little bit, to some degree—whether you smoke, because it's in tobacco, or whether you eat grapes or drink orange juice or tea.

Q: How were you able to tease out other influences, such as environmental and social factors?

A: It's an extremely hard problem in the field of genetics. One of the major limitations with these genetic associations with diet is that they're so influenced by your environment, educational attainment, socioeconomic status and income.

How do we also know whether a gene is actually impacting dietary intake or if it's another trait? A good example would be a gene that increases your risk for diabetes. When you have diabetes, you tend to change your diet in order to manage the disease. If we find a gene that links to diabetes, it's going to look like it's also associated with diet because diabetes is associated with diet.

I did an analysis that essentially takes a genetic variant that you know is strongly associated with, say, fruit intake and see if it also has an association with other traits–whether it's a health trait, such as diabetes, or a lifestyle trait, such as socioeconomic status. If the genetic variant has a stronger association with something related to the environment, health conditions or all the other outside factors that influence dietary intake, it's probably not associated with a direct mechanism, such as digestion or taste.

My goal is to find the genes that are really closely linked to dietary intake and not other conditions because I want to see if we can act on those genes' biological pathways. For instance, we could alter the flavor compound that binds to [specific receptors] to elicit a different brain response. Perhaps that could improve people's nutritional adherence to healthier foods for disease management.

Q: Where would you like the research to go next?

A: I think there's a whole slew of studies and analyses that we can do. This one is just scratching the surface. Now that we have these regions in the genome, let's figure them out and identify those genes that have a direct mechanism impact on dietary intake.

The sensory mechanisms are one of my favorites because I think that we could really use them as a tool. They tend to be these lock-and-key receptors, and if we create a different key, we might be able to alter the bindings. So I think that there's potential, scientifically, to intervene with them. One of the things I'm particularly interested in is understanding how having different genotypes, particularly of these sensory genes, changes the activation of pleasure and reward regions in the brain. I wonder if we can start creating synthetic or even natural compounds that could alter someone's pleasure reaction either to healthy or unhealthy foods–if we can use this almost as a supplement to change how people like food or not. Flavor is actually the number-one driver for food choice, even among all the other factors that influence whether someone eats certain foods or not. So can we modify the perception of flavor by understanding the biology?

There's also some room to assess whether certain foods are actually impacting different health conditions. Unfortunately, in the nutrition field, there have been a lot of studies based on correlation. They're studies that say a food is associated with lowering cholesterol, but many of those studies aren't successful in a randomized controlled trial in humans–which is really hard to do and expensive. There's a method in genetics called Mendelian randomization that mimics a randomized controlled trial, so we can test for causal and not correlative associations between different foods and different diseases. By identifying these regions in the genome that are influencing dietary intake, we can plug them into this method and get more information on what diseases certain foods actually causally influence.

About the Author

Lauren J. Young is an associate editor for health and medicine at Scientific American. *She has edited and written stories that tackle a wide range of subjects, including the COVID pandemic, emerging diseases, evolutionary biology and health inequities. Young has nearly a decade of newsroom and science journalism experience. Before joining* Scientific American *in 2023, she was an associate editor at* Popular Science *and a digital producer at public radio's* Science Friday. *She has appeared as a guest on radio shows, podcasts and stage events. Young has also spoken on panels for the Asian American Journalists Association, American Library Association, NOVA Science Studio and the New York Botanical Garden. Her work has appeared in* Scholastic MATH, School Library Journal, IEEE Spectrum, Atlas Obscura *and* Smithsonian Magazine. *Young studied biology at California Polytechnic State University, San Luis Obispo, before pursuing a master's at New York University's Science, Health & Environmental Reporting Program.*

Section 3: Nutrition and Health

Artificial Sweetener Erythritol Linked to Blood Clots, Study Warns

By Kate Graham-Shaw

Sugar-free food and drinks may not be a healthier choice after all. Used since the 1990s in everyday products from gum and candy to cookies and diet sodas, the artificial sweetener erythritol has 70 percent of the sweetness of sugar but far fewer calories. It is also commonly blended with stevia-based sweeteners to increase their volume and sweetness and give them a sugarlike texture. The Food and Drug Administration lists erythritol as safe—but in the past couple of years, experts have suggested that it may adversely affect cardiovascular health. And a study published this month in *Arteriosclerosis, Thrombosis, and Vascular Biology* has found that erythritol may be linked to an increased risk of thrombosis, the formation of vessel-blocking blood clots.

In the new study, all participants who drank a beverage containing erythritol were found to have major changes to their platelets—tiny cell fragments that flow in our blood and build up around a wound to stem bleeding. The changes included an increased tendency for platelets to clump together, says study co-author Stanley Hazen, a physician and researcher of cardiovascular medicine at Cleveland Clinic. Erythritol, he says, "increased the susceptibility of a person or their platelets for clotting and aligned with all the prior data that had been collected."

Erythritol is chemically described as a "sugar alcohol." Small amounts of it occur naturally in certain fruits and vegetables and in fermented foods, including cheese and wine. The compound is even naturally produced in some cells of the human body. But emerging evidence indicates that consuming erythritol as a sugar substitute may pose health risks. The new study builds on research by Hazen and the Cleveland Clinic team in 2023 in which blood plasma samples from more than 4,000 participants suggested a link between high erythritol levels and an increased rate of heart attacks and strokes. "This is an unrecognized concern," Hazen says. "With every cohort we look at, higher levels of erythritol are tracking with higher future risk of [cardiovascular] events."

The new study looked more closely at erythritol's effects in a smaller group of 20 healthy people. Researchers first looked at each participant's blood plasma to establish baseline platelet clumping activity. One group of 10 people then drank 30 grams of erythritol (the mean amount that an individual in the U.S. consumes per day, according to the FDA), and the other participants took 30 grams of glucose (ordinary sugar). After 30 minutes, their plasma was once again examined to determine clumping activity. Those who had consumed erythritol had a more than 1,000-fold increase of the compound in their blood—and a significant jump in platelet clotting activity. No such changes were observed in participants who had ingested glucose.

"The current data that we have is arguing that having the glucose-sweetened beverage in moderation is actually a safer choice than the erythritol-sweetened drink," Hazen says.

Inadvertent clotting can lead to huge problems in a blood vessel and potentially cause strokes, pulmonary embolisms, heart attacks and other complications. The study team is still yet to identify an underlying mechanism by which erythritol seems to boost clotting; Hazen thinks it may have something to do with "receptors on the surface of a platelet that is interacting with the erythritol." Such an interaction might alter the way platelets process signals about when to clump.

Although the recent findings raise concerns about erythritol, other experts in the field think more research is needed before considering the sweetener "unsafe."

"This study did not look at long-term exposure [to] dietary erythritol," says Duane Mellor, a registered dietician in the U.K. "It looked at the metabolic effects of a high dose in a drink and then plasma levels" only minutes after consumption. Mellor thinks it would be rash to directly link immediate heightened erythritol levels with long-term cardiovascular disease risks. "There is a large extrapolation or jump from one to another," he says. Mellor adds that "diet is not the only source of erythritol" and that the new study didn't take into account the erythritol produced by the body's normal metabolic processes.

The recent study also had a relatively small sample base; larger-scale human trials are needed to confirm the findings. Alice Lichtenstein, senior scientist and leader of the Cardiovascular Nutrition Team at the Jean Mayer USDA Human Nutrition Research Center on Aging at Tufts University, hopes for broader, more comprehensive research on multiple sweeteners to "systematically compare different nonnutritive [or artificial] sweeteners relative to each other and to sugar." Much of researchers' current knowledge, she says, is "based on different pieces of the puzzle joined together." She explains that various studies on sweeteners have used differing methods of analysis or have only considered a patchwork of effects. For example, one sweetener might be looked at for heart attack risk, whereas another might only be tested for effects on blood sugar levels. "Many times, the studies are not directly comparable," she notes.

Hazen agrees that more research is needed on both the health effects of dietary erythritol and on potentially safer alternatives. Overall, previous studies on sweeteners' benefits for losing weight and managing diabetes have had mixed results, he says. "Even [the World Health Organization is] recommending avoiding artificial sweeteners as there is not enough evidence enough to support their benefit," Hazen says. Until there are more data, he remains cautious about erythritol. "As a physician who takes care of diabetic patients and patients at risk of thrombotic events, I used to recommend artificial sweeteners," he says. "Now I tell them, 'Stay away from the artificial stuff until we know more.'"

About the Author

Kate Graham-Shaw is a journalist based in New York City. She covers international news for Japanese media and also covers health and science topics as a freelancer.

How to Know if You Have Food Poisoning, and How to Avoid It

By Kate Graham-Shaw

Thanks to the development of modern agriculture, the germ theory of disease and pasteurization, as well as the advent of freezers, electric ovens and fridges, millions of people can now access safe, disease-free food in many parts of the world. But despite these advances, foodborne illnesses endure. The Centers for Disease Control and Prevention estimates that around 48 million Americans–one in seven–get sick from food each year.

Harmful, illness-causing pathogens lurk and fester in many different foods, from salad greens, fruit and vegetables to meat, eggs, rice and seafood. Improper food preparation and storage, lack of hand hygiene, general unsanitary conditions and insufficient cooking or reheating can all lead to food contamination. A lot of foodborne illnesses are caused by such improper handling. "The vast majority will be sporadic cases," says Martin Wiedmann, a food scientist at the Cornell University College of Agriculture and Life Sciences. "One person gets sick because one thing went wrong."

It is possible for contamination to occur during growth of crops, animal agriculture and production procedures, however. Strict food hygiene laws and monitoring agencies (including the CDC, the Food and Drug Administration and the U.S. Department of Agriculture's Food Safety and Inspection Service) ensure that the U.S. has one of the best food safety records in the world. But unexpected events or mistakes on farms or in factories can still lead to foodborne pathogen contamination. When outbreaks of foodborne illnesses do happen, experts can use DNA fingerprinting of bacteria to quickly identify the origin and recall any food that might be contaminated, helping to contain the spread.

Common symptoms of foodborne illness include upset stomach, nausea, vomiting, diarrhea, fatigue and fever. In severe cases, people can be hospitalized and die. Pregnant women, elderly adults, immunocompromised individuals and young children are more susceptible to foodborne illnesses. Around 30 percent of all foodborne illness deaths worldwide occur in children under five years old.

The CDC recognizes 31 pathogens as common sources of foodborne illness. Bacteria, viruses, chemicals and even parasites (such as tapeworms) can all be culprits. These are some of the major microbes you should especially watch out for.

E. coli

Escherichia coli bacteria normally live peacefully inside your intestines without harming you. If ingested, however, these bacteria can infect other areas of the body, causing diarrhea, vomiting and stomach pain. Some severe strains (such as those that produce so-called Shiga toxin) can lead to life-threatening dehydration and serious kidney damage.

E. coli can be expelled from the intestines in feces, meaning that unsanitary bathroom conditions and poor hygiene habits can all cause contamination of food. If a person gets such bacteria on their hands from direct or indirect contact with fecal matter, and then they go to prepare food or handle kitchen utensils with unwashed hands, for example, the *E. coli* can easily spread and become foodborne. Unclean water and unpasteurized beverages (such as raw milk) can also spread *E. coli*. Farmed produce also carries an *E. coli* risk–particularly if wildlife or livestock feces come into contact with the bacterium.

"*E. coli* is often associated with cattle and other ruminants," says Martin Bucknavage, food safety and quality specialist at the Pennsylvania State University's Penn Extension, which focuses on agriculture. "It could be cows, sheep, even white-tailed deer–it's in their intestinal tract." Contamination can occur if an infected animal's feces get into water supplies and crops. This route is thought to have caused a number of *E. coli* outbreaks in produce, such as one in spinach in 2006. But this type of pathogen exposure has decreased in recent years, partly because farmers have been better at controlling livestock waste, Bucknavage says. "The meat industry has done a lot of work to try to minimize it."

Salmonella

Salmonella bacteria are most often associated with raw chicken and eggs, and ingesting food contaminated with them can lead to symptoms such as fever, diarrhea and stomach cramps. The bacterium is estimated to infect more than one million people in the U.S. every year.

"Big industry has a lot of strategies in place to reduce the risk of *Salmonella*," Wiedmann says. But eating certain foods raw or unprocessed, such as raw eggs or unpasteurized milk, can cause outbreaks, including the recent Raw Farm milk company outbreak this year. In addition to eggs, unpasteurized milk and raw chicken, foods from which people have gotten sick include peanut butter, raw pork, raw beef and cucumbers. Raw flour can also be a source of *salmonella* infection, so people should avoid consuming raw cookie dough and cake mix.

Like *E. coli*, *Salmonella* lives in the intestines of humans and other animals and can be caught through contact with feces. It can also be found on the skin and fur of many animals, especially in warm climates. "A lot of our food supplies are coming from these warmer areas where there's a lot of wildlife," especially lizards, Bucknavage says. "So it can get onto crops that way."

Birds, hedgehogs, turtles, guinea pigs and even pet bearded dragons can all carry *Salmonella* and cause contamination through direct or indirect contact.

Listeria

Named after Joseph Lister, a British surgeon who pioneered the use of antiseptics in surgery, *Listeria* is another genus of bacteria that can potentially cause nasty infections if ingested. Preventing *Listeria* contamination can be a challenge, Bucknavage says. "It's one that has the ability to grow at refrigeration temperatures," he adds. *Listeria* contamination is especially difficult for manufacturers to prevent.

"Companies go to great lengths to try to control it within those processing environments," Bucknavage explains. But despite these efforts, *Listeria* outbreaks can still occur. The deli meat brand Boar's Head recently recalled millions of pounds of meat after foodborne *Listeria* caused at least two deaths and several dozen hospitalizations across more than a dozen states. "It has a high mortality rate compared to other pathogens," Bucknavage says. "If it enters the bloodstream, it can lead to a blood infection, or septicemia, or it can infect your neural system, leading to things like meningitis," or inflammation of the brain and spinal cord.

Infected people can experience aches, diarrhea and vomiting. High fever, severe headache, confusion, neck stiffness and sensitivity to light are all signs of bacterial meningitis, and people with these symptoms should seek medical care immediately.

Despite the horrible effects the bacteria have when ingested, recent research has been looking at the possibility of using *Listeria* as a cancer vaccine. This research is in its early stages, however, and *Listeria* is still very harmful in its unaltered, foodborne state.

Norovirus

Norovirus is a genus of very contagious viruses that can cause nausea, vomiting, diarrhea and stomach pain. These symptoms start around 12 to 48 hours after infection and usually last one to three days. Colloquially known as a "stomach bug" or "stomach flu," this foodborne illness is estimated to sicken around one in 15 people in the U.S. each year.

"*Norovirus* is one that easily spreads throughout a population," Bucknavage says. And people themselves, rather than food production, are typically the culprit. "Somebody goes to work, and they're ill, and then they handle food, and it spreads very easily, person to person [or] person to food."

Part of the Caliciviridae family of viruses, *Norovirus* causes the stomach and intestines to swell, initiating gastroenteritis. The viral illness usually runs its course in a few days, but it's important to drink plenty of fluids to stay hydrated. You should seek medical help if you're a member of a vulnerable group or if your symptoms don't improve.

How Can You Avoid Foodborne Illness?

Fortunately, a major way to help prevent becoming infected is pretty simple: wash your hands with warm water and soap before preparing, cooking and eating food. Doing so after using the bathroom, picking up dog waste or changing diapers is also important, as is carefully cleaning food preparation surfaces, cutlery and chopping boards after they've come into contact with raw meat.

Meat thermometers are also great tools to help you tell if food has reached the necessary temperature to kill most microbes. The temperature needed to heat certain meats and fish can vary. The USDA recommends reheating food to an internal temperature of at least 165 degrees Fahrenheit (74 degrees Celsius).

There are the four basic practices to avoid infection from foodborne illnesses, Wiedmann says: "cooking, chilling, [avoiding] cross contamination, cleaning or washing your hands right before you prepare food." The CDC emphasizes these "four steps to food safety." Wiedmann notes, "If you combine those four things, you can substantially reduce your risk of foodborne illness."

What to Do if You Have Food Poisoning

Hydration is vital when you think you're dealing with foodborne illness. Healthy adults often find their symptoms get better after several days. But if the symptoms persist or the sick person is from a vulnerable group, medical attention might be necessary. The CDC recommends that individuals seek medical advice if they have the following symptoms: bloody diarrhea, fever above 102 degrees F (39 degrees C), diarrhea lasting more than three days, frequent vomiting and severe dehydration.

About the Author

Kate Graham-Shaw is a journalist based in New York City. She covers international news for Japanese media and also covers health and science topics as a freelancer.

People with Food Allergies Can Treat Symptoms with Asthma Medication, FDA Decides

By Andrew Chapman

Any time people with severe allergies to foods such as peanuts, milk or eggs sit down for a meal–whether at home, a friend's place or a restaurant–they must pay careful attention to each ingredient they're eating. Two children in every U.S. classroom and nearly 11 percent of adults have a food allergy and thus must be constantly vigilant. For some, even a trace of the allergen on a fork or spoon could trigger a life-threatening reaction.

Now the drug omalizumab, developed by the company Genentech as an asthma treatment and sold under the name Xolair, has been approved by the U.S. Food and Drug Administration as an injectable treatment for certain food allergies. The study that led to approval was published this week in the *New England Journal of Medicine*. It showed that the monoclonal antibody treatment quelled allergic reactions in around two thirds of people with allergies to foods that included peanuts, milk and eggs. The results suggest Xolair won't completely rid people of their allergies–or make it safe for them to eat those foods in large quantities–but it could provide an important safety net in case of accidental consumption or exposure.

"This drug will reduce the anxiety our patients have around doing everyday things that people without food allergies take for granted," says Sharon Chinthrajah, an allergist and immunologist at Stanford University and senior author of the study.

Food allergies develop when the body wrongfully identifies food proteins as a threat. Many such allergies involve a type of antibody (a protein that allows the immune system to find and neutralize invaders) called immunoglobulin E, or IgE. When the immune system detects a food allergen, it produces IgE, which binds to protective immune cells in the blood. IgE then seeks out and grabs hold of the food protein, triggering the still attached immune cells to flood the body with inflammation-causing histamines and other chemicals. These chemicals prompt allergic symptoms such as hives, swelling of the lips and anaphylaxis–a dangerous whole-body reaction that causes low blood pressure and difficulty breathing. Xolair effectively dulls IgE's ability to initiate the inflammatory response; it does this by blocking the antibody from binding to the immune cells.

In the new study, researchers used a randomized controlled trial to test the drug's efficacy on 177 children and adolescents at 10 medical centers across the U.S. All participants were allergic to peanuts and two other foods, such as cashews, walnuts, hazelnuts, eggs, milk or wheat.

Two thirds of the participants received a Xolair injection every two to four weeks during the trial, depending on their weight and IgE levels, while the remaining individuals received a placebo. After four to five months of treatment–and under close medical supervision–each participant ate a small amount of peanut protein, equivalent to about four peanuts. Two thirds of the participants who had received the drug showed no symptoms of an allergic reaction, but 93 percent of those who took the placebo did. Similar results emerged for most of the other foods tested, though Xolair appeared to protect only 41 percent of people with a cashew allergy. Chinthrajah doesn't know why cashews might be different. She notes, however, that participants with this allergy did report improvements the longer they were on the drug.

Because Xolair blocks all forms of IgE, whether specific to proteins in nuts, milk or eggs, the researchers also wanted to test whether the drug could prevent allergic reactions to multiple foods simultaneously. The scientists had children eat small amounts of two or three foods they were allergic to at the same time and found that at the four-peanut-equivalent dose, most could tolerate two of the foods, and nearly half could consume three without a reaction. "This is nicely shown in the trial," says Maria Curotto De Lafaille, an immunologist at the Icahn School of Medicine at Mount Sinai, who wasn't involved in the research. She notes that this test was important, given that children with one food allergy have a higher risk of developing more.

The drug also worked for children of different ages, including those as young as one year. "So no matter what age you're diagnosed or what age you're seeking treatment, this has a good probability of being effective," Chinthrajah says.

Chinthrajah emphasizes that people using Xolair can still experience allergic reactions; the drug only helped raise the threshold for how much allergen the study participants could tolerate. When the researchers bumped up the test doses, more children showed signs of a reaction. "Our patients still need to be very careful," she says. The treatment regimen may also be a considerable barrier to some children and adults because a shot is needed every two to four weeks and must be administered by a health-care worker. The doctors who ran the study plan to offer a self-injection option that can be administered at home, similar to the Xolair asthma treatment. But for some children, particularly those with needle phobias, this might not be appropriate.

The drug's price, around $1,500 per injection, could also deter families without comprehensive insurance. Many insurance companies cover Xolair as an asthma treatment, and Chinthrajah hopes this will hold once doctors start prescribing it for food allergies.

Only one other immunotherapy, called Palforzia, is currently FDA-approved for peanut allergies in children between four and 17 years old. Palforzia is a tiny, repeated dose of peanut protein that is taken orally. Over time this gradually shifts the immune system away from recognizing the protein as a threat and producing IgE. As with Xolair, people who use Palforzia for their peanut allergy still need to avoid peanuts. Lafaille notes that "one of the problems with oral immunotherapy is that there are a lot of reactions, even anaphylaxis," in response to the treatment itself. By comparison, children who took Xolair and those who took the placebo experienced a similar number of adverse reactions. (Xolair does have a 0.2 percent rate of anaphylaxis, and the medication comes with a boxed warning.)

Other promising allergy drugs block interleukins, which are immune chemicals that stimulate the production of IgE in response to an allergenic food. But so far none have been FDA-approved for food allergies.

The clinical trial of Xolair for food allergies is still underway, and the results reported so far have "opened up the door to so many more questions," Chinthrajah says. In the next stages of testing, the researchers want to combine the drug with Palforzia to see if doing so will offer greater protection. They also want to test children's tolerance to allergenic foods after stopping Xolair to check whether the drug has long-lasting impacts on the immune system.

Such future research could guide scientists in tailoring Xolair allergy therapy for individual people. Chinthrajah says the drug, as currently approved, can already provide substantial benefits—especially for allergies so severe that a tiny, accidental exposure can be life-threatening. "Hopefully," she says, they can "live life a little freer."

About the Author

Andrew Chapman is a Truckee, Calif.–based freelance science writer who covers life sciences and the environment.

Can Coffee's Effects on Appetite and Digestion Cause Weight Loss?

By Lori Youmshajekian

After sipping a morning cup of coffee, most people are jolted awake. Others might notice that the drink tames their hunger, too. Many people on social media are increasingly drinking their favorite pick-me-up to shed pounds. But studies are only beginning to unravel how caffeine and other compounds in coffee might affect weight.

Several dieting trends and recipes categorized under the nickname "the coffee loophole" have picked up steam since early this year, stirring a renewed interest in consuming coffee (or caffeine in general) to lose weight. These sources claim that adding household spices or commercial supplements to a cup of joe or even chugging the mixture within seven seconds of experiencing a hunger pang can enhance the weight-loss effect. Experts are still puzzling over this: Does coffee–and particularly caffeine–contribute to people losing pounds in the first place? And how long do any weight-loss effects last?

Coffee and other caffeine products have been rumored to be a quick, easy weight-loss fix. The rationale is partly linked to coffee's ability to get the digestive system moving. The caffeine in coffee can ramp up muscle contractions in the colon that stimulate bowel movements. That means the digestive system clears its contents a little quicker than usual. Caffeine is also a diuretic, meaning it increases urine production, and peeing more causes a loss of water weight. These combined effects on digestion and water weight happen quickly after consuming coffee but are short-lived–they don't cause permanent weight loss. Consuming coffee over longer periods of time, however, seems to bring on different effects.

Drinking coffee regularly doesn't lead to significant weight *loss*, but it may prevent weight *gain*–albeit modestly. The average person typically gains weight as they get older–about a pound per year through middle age–but avid coffee drinkers seem to experience less age-related weight gain. A 2023 study followed the coffee habits of more than 150,000 participants and found that drinking unsweetened coffee was associated with a modest reduction in weight gain over four years after adjusting for other lifestyle variables. With each additional cup, the coffee drinkers gained about a quarter of a pound less than their peers. Most people probably won't feel such a small difference in weight, though. Other studies have reported similar results. "You're still gaining weight; it's just slightly less compared to the general population," explains Frank Hu, chair of the department of nutrition at the Harvard T. H. Chan School of Public Health and co-author of the 2023 paper.

Coffee has also been linked to a small loss of body fat. In one study, people who drank four cups of instant coffee a day had 4 percent less fat mass. They also lost a small amount of their total weight after a period of almost six months. That's compared with a placebo group that drank a beverage that looked and tasted like coffee and maintained similar diet and exercise habits.

Caffeine, the primary bioactive compound in coffee, appears to be one of the main drivers of the reduced weight gain. The compound is known to stimulate diet-induced thermogenesis–the energy used to digest, absorb and store nutrients from food. On average, people spend about 10 percent of their total energy expenditure processing food. Studies have shown that caffeine can increase that amount by raising a person's metabolic rate. A higher metabolic rate causes the body to use more energy at rest. The digestive process speeds up, causing organs in the gut to use slightly more energy and burn more calories. Overall, this energy increase is small, however: coffee drinkers might burn 80 to 150 more calories per day, according to one short-term study. That's equivalent to a few Oreo cookies–but those few extra lost calories can add up over time, Hu says.

Caffeine is also believed to stimulate the sympathetic nervous system, which regulates the body's fight-or-flight response. It blocks receptors that bind adenosine, a neurotransmitter that triggers feelings of sleepiness and promotes relaxation. Caffeine then prompts physiological responses in the sympathetic nervous system such as increased heart rate and alertness. That, in turn, burns slightly more calories, explains Marilyn Cornelis, an associate professor of preventive medicine at Northwestern University. Caffeine may also increase fat oxidation—the process of breaking down fat stored in tissues for energy—which might explain why coffee consumption is associated with a decrease in fat mass.

Independent of caffeine, coffee also contains several polyphenols—a type of antioxidant—that might affect weight. Chlorogenic acid, the polyphenol that gives coffee its distinctly bitter taste and strong aroma, has been shown to help maintain stable blood glucose levels. Because food cravings can be related to blood sugar fluctuations, more stable blood sugar might also help regulate appetite, Cornelis says. The bitter taste itself could also play a role; there's evidence that the gut senses bitter compounds and adjusts appetite hormones to reduce food intake.

Scientists are only beginning to understand how chlorogenic acid may enhance coffee's effect on hormones that control appetite and hunger. One small study that followed 126 people who were considered overweight found that coffee had a regulatory effect on satiety hormones; people ate slightly less and felt fuller after drinking the beverage. After drinking coffee, participants had higher levels of serotonin, a brain chemical that, among other things, can suppress appetite, and lower levels of the hunger-inducing hormone ghrelin. These effects were stronger in those who drank the coffee blend that contained more chlorogenic acid. The evidence suggests that coffee might influence appetite and hunger, but it may vary immensely from person to person. So drinking coffee to immediately suppress a spike in hunger may not be a realistic expectation. Scientists are also still trying to understand whether additives such as cinnamon and cayenne pepper tangibly contribute to coffee's modest weight-loss effects, but they say those ingredients are harmless to add.

Coffee's effects on health overall appear to be beneficial—in moderation. Research has consistently linked long-term coffee consumption to a lower risk of type 2 diabetes, heart disease, improved cognitive function and even lower mortality. But upping coffee intake simply to achieve these effects isn't right for everyone. "It's not like more is better," says Rob van Dam, a professor in exercise and nutrition sciences at the George Washington University. Drinking more than about 400 milligrams of caffeine per day might cause difficulty sleeping, more stress and some anxiety, he says. To put that in perspective, one shot of espresso typically has about 60 milligrams of caffeine, though popular coffee beverages can contain much more, depending on size and roast.

Flavored lattes or frappes high in sugar and cream counteract some of the benefits that black coffee has on weight management. "That's kind of a no-brainer," Cornelis says. "Sugar adds calories, and coffee is traditionally a calorie-free beverage." She suggests drinking coffee with less sugar and cream instead.

Hu says that, overall, coffee may have a modest benefit for weight loss but advises against "unrealistic expectations that drinking a lot of coffee ... will dramatically change your body weight."

About the Author

Lori Youmshajekian is a freelance science journalist who reports on advances in health, environmental issues and scientific misconduct. She holds a master's degree in Science Journalism from New York University and has written for New Scientist, Yale E360, Retraction Watch *and* Medscape, *among other outlets.*

Some Sugar Substitutes Affect Blood Glucose and Gut Bacteria

By Emily Willingham

As Diet Coke and its sweetener aspartame wrap up 40 years or so on American store shelves, the decades-long controversy around the safety of sugar substitutes continues. Ever since diet drinks hit the stores in the 1950s, rumors have swirled that such sweeteners–which today also include saccharin, sucralose and stevia–do more than satisfy a sweet tooth without the calories of sugar. But whether that "more" exists hasn't been easy to establish.

In a new study of four sugar substitutes, researchers found that these nonnutritive sweeteners don't just travel through the body unnoticed. The study results, published on August 19 in *Cell*, link two of the sweeteners–saccharin and sucralose–to spikes in glucose levels and suggest all four are tied to a shift in gut microbe profiles. Whether these findings translate into trouble, benefit or neither remains to be seen, and aficionados of diet drinks don't need to trash the diet soda can just yet.

"It's cool science and was very well designed, thought out and executed," says Dylan Mackay, an assistant professor of nutrition and chronic disease at the University of Manitoba, who was not involved in the study. "I've always wanted to do these more at-home trials, and they were able to pull it off in a really interesting way."

In 2014 researchers found a link between microbiome changes and blood glucose responses in mice after intake of sugar substitutes. To see if those same links applied to humans in the new study, the scientists selected participants from a potential pool of more than 1,375 people, ruling out anyone who consumed noncaloric sweeteners in their regular daily life. Some had unknowingly done so by way of protein powders, chewing gum, or low-sugar snacks or desserts.

The researchers split the final 120 participants into six groups of 20. In four of these groups, participants consumed commercial packets of one of the four sweeteners at levels below their federal daily limit. A fifth group consumed only the filler used in these packets, which is commonly added to bulk out the tiny amount of sugar substitute they contain. The sixth group had no intervention.

During the two weeks that participants consumed their assigned sweetener or the filler, they also took oral glucose tolerance tests, which are used to measure the body's response to sugar and can be employed to diagnose some forms of diabetes. For these tests, they drank a glucose solution every morning after overnight fasting and used home-based continuous glucose monitors to track their blood glucose levels. The researchers also collected oral and stool samples from the participants to analyze the species of microbes they hosted. Study investigators additionally measured levels of some products of metabolism in the blood.

The participants who consumed saccharin or sucralose had a steeper blood glucose response than any of the other groups. When participants consumed any of the four sugar substitutes, their gut bacteria profile changed during the two weeks of intake. Along with these changes, levels of the metabolic products changed, too. For example, in participants who took saccharin, the production of a type of amino acid increased,echoing patterns seen in people with diabetes.

To confirm a link between microbial profiles and blood glucose responses, the investigators orally administered microbiomes–taken from the human participants with the highest and lowest blood glucose spikes following sweetener consumption–to germ-free mice. Mice exposed to microbiomes from human "top responders" showed changes in their blood glucose that "very significantly mirrored those of the donor individuals," says study author Eran Elinav, principal investigator of the Host-Microbiome Interaction Research Group at the Weizmann Institute of Science in Rehovot, Israel, and director of the Microbiome and Cancer Division at the German National Cancer Center in Heidelberg.

This part of the work "is a really cool portion of the paper," Mackay says. The findings in mice "are interesting mechanistic evidence that maybe [these sweeteners] are having an effect."

The effects of the sweeteners on blood glucose are likely highly personalized, Elinav says. But the results suggest these compounds don't just pass through the body, as some originally thought.

Part of the personalized response will relate to the health of the person involved, Mackay says. The findings "can't extend to people who may be overweight or have obesity or impaired glucose tolerance or type 1 or type 2 diabetes," he says.

The findings don't settle the question of whether any effects will be meaningful for human health–a subject to tackle in other studies, Elinav says. The researchers also don't know if these effects will persist beyond the two weeks of exposure in the current study, Mackay says.

The study involved healthy people without overweight or obesity and who represent only a subset of the population that consumes food and drink with these sugar substitutes, Mackay notes. "From a user perspective, as someone with type 1 diabetes, almost everything I use has aspartame," he says. "I'm not going to stop that and switch back to regular glucose or sugar-containing products because of these results."

About the Author

Emily Willingham is a science writer and author of the books Phallacy: Life Lessons from the Animal Penis *(Avery, Penguin Publishing Group, 2020) and* The Tailored Brain: From Ketamine, to Keto, to Companionship: A User's Guide to Feeling Better and Thinking Smarter *(Basic Books, 2021).*

How Do Ultraprocessed Foods Affect Your Health?

By Lori Youmshajekian

You might think you know a processed meal when you see one, but here's some food for thought: nearly every edible thing at the supermarket has undergone some kind of processing, such as washing, blanching, canning, drying or pasteurizing. In other words, if there is any change from the way the food begins to the way it ends up on a shelf, it counts as processed.

But then there are *ultraprocessed* foods. Both frozen chopped spinach and canned sausages are processed, but the latter have been through much more processing than the former. Ultraprocessed foods undergo an industrial process in their journey from farm to table. This often includes steps such as hydrogenation, which produces semisolid oils, and hydrolysis, which enhances flavors. These foods also contain a variety of additives that help to bind the ingredients together, increase their shelf life or make them more palatable.

According to some estimates, nearly 60 percent of the daily calories U.S. adults consume are from ultraprocessed foods. It's worse for kids and teenagers, whose diets are almost 70 percent ultraprocessed.

But a growing number of studies have linked higher consumption of ultraprocessed foods to a long list of health effects, and scientists are beginning to understand why.

What Are Ultraprocessed Foods?

Chicken nuggets, chips and hot dogs are considered ultraprocessed, but so are things such as fruit yogurts, mass produced bread and even some canned foods. As a rule of thumb, an ultraprocessed food is one that cannot be made in an ordinary kitchen–in other words, it contains at least one ingredient that is not typically found in homes or has undergone an industrial process that a home cook would not be able to replicate.

"A whole lot of things that you could never imagine can be done [to food]," says Barry Popkin, a professor of nutrition at the University of North Carolina at Chapel Hill. "You can't tell simply by the ingredients." For example, he says, "it'll be flour, but you really don't know that wheat flour has been decomposed in such complex ways and then put back together."

Researchers commonly use a four-part classification known as NOVA to group foods based on the extent of industrial processing they involve. The categories are unprocessed or minimally processed foods (which include vegetables and eggs), processed culinary ingredients (those that are usually added to food and rarely eaten alone, such as oils, butter and sugar), processed foods (those that are made from a combination of the first two groups, such as homemade bread), and ultraprocessed foods (those that are made with industrially modified raw ingredients and additives).

When NOVA was first introduced in 2009, it offered a new way of looking at food beyond its nutritional value. Take fortified breads or protein-rich cookies, for example: Compared with their unfortified equivalents, they would be considered relatively nutritious. But through the lens of NOVA, both are ultraprocessed.

Other researchers, such as Julie Hess, a nutritionist at the U.S. Department of Agriculture's Agricultural Research Service and former vice president of scientific affairs at the National Dairy Council, contend that NOVA is not the best or most consistent way to identify an ultraprocessed food. She argues that ultraprocessed foods are not all the same in terms of nutrition. "When we say 'ultraprocessed food,' are we going to include things like canned beans? Are we including canned oranges and dried peaches?" Hess asks. "That question of nutrient density isn't currently reflected in the NOVA categorization system."

Popkin and his colleagues looked at other ways to identify foods as ultraprocessed in an April 2024 paper. He says having at least one of 12 types of additives–including specific flavors, emulsifiers, foams, thickening agents and glazing agents–as an ingredient is a feature of all ultraprocessed foods. The presence of artificial coloring or flavoring would be a telltale sign for about 97 percent of these foods, he says.

Are Ultraprocessed Foods Bad for Your Health?

Many people believe that eating ultraprocessed food will make them gain weight or cause a host of other health issues, and some evidence backs this idea up. Research has tied the consumption of ultraprocessed foods to a slew of health conditions, including obesity, type 2 diabetes, some cancers, cardiovascular disease, and even mild depression and anxiety, but a clear mechanism for harm hasn't been identified.

A landmark paper in 2019 was the first to show a cause-and-effect link between ultraprocessed foods and weight gain. A group of 20 healthy volunteers was confined to a ward at the National Institutes of Health Clinical Center in Bethesda, Md., where the participants were randomly assigned to receive a diet of either ultraprocessed or minimally processed food for two weeks and then were switched to the other diet for the next two weeks. For example, a person receiving the ultraprocessed diet would start their day with foods such as packaged cereal and a blueberry muffin or croissants and turkey sausages. Someone eating the minimally processed diet would instead receive Greek yogurt and fruit or a fresh omelet and sweet potato hash.

On average, people eating the ultraprocessed diet consumed about 500 calories more per day, compared with those fed the minimally processed diet. Participants in the former group also ate faster and gained about two pounds after two weeks. On the minimally processed diet, participants ate less and lost about the same amount of weight as they gained on the processed diet. In both settings, participants were given access to about double the number of calories they needed and were told to eat as much as they wanted.

Kevin Hall, the study's lead author and a clinical researcher at the National Institute of Diabetes and Digestive and Kidney Diseases, says he designed the investigation because he thought the NOVA classification system–which doesn't account for the nutrients contained in different foods–was "nonsense." He matched foods in the two diets so that they had the same total amount of nutrients, including fat, carbohydrates and fiber, "because I thought the nutrients were going to drive the effects," Hall says. "And I was wrong."

Hess, who was not involved in the study, notes some limitations. There were "very, very different" foods in the two groups, she says–in other words, the study didn't match the diets for quality. Hall says the two diets used different foods because it would have been "very difficult to make homemade versions of many popular ultraprocessed foods while maintaining precise control over their nutrition content." Hess's lab designed a diet in which 90 percent of the calories were from ultraprocessed foods, and it still met most national guidelines for nutrients–calling into question how useful NOVA is for determining the healthfulness of a food when existing dietary guidelines are used as a benchmark.

Others say findings such as Hall's study suggest that processing may change how a food affects our body, independent of the nutrients that food contains. "It goes to show how much the [U.S. dietary] guidelines are focused on nutrients," says Filippa Juul, a nutritional epidemiologist at New York University. "You could have any food and just tune up the nutrients; it doesn't mean the food is necessarily healthy ... or has the same activity as nutrients that are in [unprocessed] foods."

Studies have also suggested a link between higher consumption of ultraprocessed foods and a profound change in the composition of gut microbes. And an altered gut microbiome has been linked to mental health conditions. The negative effects of these foods might also be a result of what they lack: fiber. The act of industrially processing a food can lower its fiber content, which can make it less filling. Fiber also feeds bacteria in the gut, and the absence of this nutrient may explain the links among diet, depression and gut health, too.

"There are probably some subcategories [of ultraprocessed foods] that are perfectly fine—maybe even really good for you—and others that are particularly damaging," Hall says. "I just don't think we know which ones [are which]." Part of the problem with ultraprocessed foods is that they're often packed with calories yet leave us craving more.

Why Do We Like Ultraprocessed Foods So Much?

Scientists still don't know for sure why humans gravitate toward ultraprocessed foods. One hypothesis, according to Hall, is that we might not be able to resist their combination of ingredients. Think about the last time you ate just one chip out of a bag—it's almost impossible not to eat more.

In a 2021 study, Hall attempted to compare a low-carbohydrate diet with a high-carbohydrate one to examine their effects on energy intake. When people were presented with meals that were high in both fat and sugar, fat and salt, or carbohydrates and salt, people tended to eat more calories, he says. "These are so-called hyperpalatable foods," Hall adds.

Such foods essentially have artificially enhanced palatability that exceeds the palatability any ingredient could produce on its own—in other words, they have a combination of fat, salt and sugar "that would never exist in nature," Juul says. Previous research showed that foods combining fat and carbohydrates were better at activating the brain's reward system than foods with just one of those ingredients. The ultraprocessed meals in Hall's study also had more calories per bite than the minimally processed foods.

Some researchers hypothesize that certain foods are addictive. People don't lose control over eating bananas, but with ultraprocessed foods, they show all the hallmarks of addiction, says Ashley Gearhardt, a professor of psychology at the University of Michigan. Addictive drugs activate the striatal dopamine system–the brain's pleasure center–by creating a dopamine spike followed by a rapid crash. "It's like a quick hit that isn't sustaining," Gearhardt observes. Ultraprocessed foods resemble nicotine and ethanol in the magnitude of that effect in the brain.

"That makes sense because the reward system of the brain was really shaped by the need to get calories," Gearhardt says. The addictive agent in food could be one of many things, she says, or some combination of them–taste, smell, sugar, fat and additives are all potential culprits. Studies in animals have shown that stopping the consumption of ultraprocessed foods elicits withdrawal symptoms such as anxiety and agitation, similar to what happens when people quit other addictive substances.

Should Ultraprocessed Food Be Regulated?

There are people who want to do away with ultraprocessed foods altogether and others who say there are not enough data to warrant any action, according to Hall. "It's not realistic to say, 'Well, we're just going to cut out 50 percent of the food,'" he says. "Who's going to make everybody's meals?" Ultraprocessed foods are a lot cheaper and more convenient than less processed ones, Hall says. In his study, the minimally processed meals cost 40 percent more to buy and took the chefs longer to prepare.

Spending hours hunched over a kitchen bench to churn butter is not the answer. But reducing consumption of ultraprocessed foods doesn't mean we have to make everything from scratch.

"There's an enormous number of things you can do," says Popkin, who eats unprocessed foods apart from an occasional iced tea sweetened with the sugar substitute Splenda. "There's a hell of a lot of packaged real food out there." He suggests looking for minimally processed options that make cooking faster, such as a salad mix or chopped vegetables.

We have to do our best to make healthy choices, Gearhardt says, but everything is stacked against us. As a food scientist, even she leaves the grocery store befuddled. "It's easy to say we should just tell the individual to do better, [but] everything in the environment is set up for the industry to profit," she says.

In an ideal world, we would focus on making healthy alternatives convenient and affordable and reducing marketing to kids, Gearhardt says. "We need to take some courageous action and have some common sense that this food environment is not good for anybody," she adds.

About the Author

Lori Youmshajekian is a freelance science journalist who reports on advances in health, environmental issues and scientific misconduct. She holds a master's degree in Science Journalism from New York University and has written for New Scientist, Yale E360, Retraction Watch *and* Medscape, *among other outlets.*

Ozempic Quiets Food Noise in the Brain—But How?

By Lauren J. Young

Kimberly Chauche, a corporate secretary in Lincoln, Neb., says she's always been overweight. When she was as young as five years old, her doctors started trying to figure out why. Since then, her life has involved nutritionists and personal trainers, and eventually she sought therapists to treat her compulsive eating and weight-related anxiety. Yet answers never arrived, and solutions never lasted.

At 43, Chauche was prescribed a weight-loss medication called Wegovy—one of a new class of drugs that mimic a hormone responsible for insulin production. She took her first dose in March 2024, injecting it into herself with a needle. Within a couple of months she had lost almost 20 pounds, and that felt great. But the weight loss seemed like a bonus compared with a startling change in how she reacted to food.

She noticed the shift almost immediately: One day her son was eating popcorn, a snack she could never resist, and she walked right past the bowl. "All of a sudden it was like some part of my brain that was always there just went quiet," she says. Her eating habits improved, and her anxiety eased. "It felt almost surreal to put an injector against my leg and have happen in 48 hours what decades of intervention could not accomplish," she says. "If I had lost almost no weight, just to have my brain working the way it's working, I would stay on this medication forever."

Chauche is hardly alone in her effusive descriptions of how Wegovy vanquished her intrusive thoughts about food an experience increasingly referred to as the "quieting of food noise." Researchers—some of whom ushered in the development of these blockbuster drugs—want to understand why.

Among them is biochemist Svetlana Mojsov of the Rockefeller University, who has spent about 50 years investigating gut hormones that could be key to regulating blood glucose levels. In seeking potential treatments for type 2 diabetes, Mojsov ultimately focused on one hormone: glucagonlike peptide 1, or GLP-1. Her sequence of the protein in the 1980s became the initial template for drugs like Wegovy. The medications, called GLP-1 receptor agonists, use a synthetic version of the natural substance to activate the hormone's receptors. The first ones arrived in 2005. In 2017 the U.S. Food and Drug Administration approved semaglutide–now widely known as Ozempic.

In the years since Ozempic came to market, GLP-1 drugs have catapulted to stardom, becoming a multibillion-dollar industry with a surreal series of successes, first as an effective treatment for diabetes and then as a hit for weight loss. Wegovy, a version of semaglutide specifically for weight loss, became available in 2021. Both drugs were created by Novo Nordisk; other pharmaceutical companies have developed similar ones. One 2024 survey in the U.S. found that one in eight adults reported having taken a GLP-1 drug.

Mojsov and other researchers know that these drugs make people lose weight because they reduce appetite and thus food intake. They make people feel fuller, faster. But scientists don't have a technical definition for so-called food noise, and they are only beginning to understand how synthetic GLP-1 acts not just in the digestive system but in the brain. This work is illuminating neurobiological explanations for hunger and satiety, pleasure and reward–as well as why these sensations so critical to survival might get dysregulated, causing compulsive behaviors and addictive patterns. "That's what we need to understand now," Mojsov says. "The next frontier is to understand the biology behind the Ozempic effects on the brain."

GLP-1 is one of many essential gut hormones that help to control eating behavior, nutritional absorption, digestion, and the overall balance of energy coming into and being used by the body. Over the past few decades several hormones from various body systems involved in food intake have been targeted as potential treatments for obesity and diabetes, but "GLP-1 seems to be the one that's risen to the top, at least for pharmacotherapy," says Scott

Kanoski, a behavioral neuroscientist and professor at the University of Southern California.

That's in part because it belongs to a batch of hormones called incretins, which prompt insulin production in response to food ingestion. In a 1987 study, Mojsov and her collaborators injected GLP-1 into a rat pancreas model to see whether it stimulated insulin secretion. "It was a beautifully clear-cut result," Mojsov says. "As the GLP-1 levels went up, insulin levels went up."

Graphic shows how the hormone GLP-1 transmits signals to the brain to influence satiety and food intake. Ozempic is a drug called semaglutide–a synthetic mimic of GLP-1 that can result in weight loss by causing people to feel full and therefore eat less.

The basic pathway of GLP-1 in the gut goes like this: When a person eats a meal, a cascade of hormones, including GLP-1, is released to aid food absorption and digestion. As the food gets broken down into glucose and other molecules in the digestive tract, GLP-1 gets released from the intestine. Levels of the hormone rise slowly, then spike to signal fullness.

Some GLP-1 in circulating blood binds directly to receptors in the pancreas to prompt the release of insulin. The hormone also can latch on to receptors on the vagus nerve–a long cranial nerve that shuttles messages between the brain and organs throughout the body. While a person eats, hormonal messages traveling via the vagus nerve tell their pancreas to produce insulin, which converts glucose to energy and brings blood glucose levels back down. The rise and fall of blood sugar can influence hunger and satiety.

GLP-1 is short-lived in its natural form. Within one or two minutes the molecule gets dismantled by enzymes in the blood and cleared by the kidneys. So in the 1990s drug companies began creating synthetic versions of GLP-1, hoping to land on a durable, longer-lasting structure. Scientists found success in a compound in Gila monster saliva that is similar to human GLP-1 but much more stable. They attached a long chain of lipids that can bind to albumin–a protein in blood that serves as a carrier for the drug–and keep the compound active for hours or even days.

Around 2021 the story of GLP-1 receptor agonists took a dramatic turn. Demand for the drugs soared as celebrities and social media influencers began sharing their experiences using Ozempic off-label to achieve incredible weight loss. As more and more people took the drugs, stories spread about "food noise," and researchers started looking even more closely at what was going on in the brain.

Matthew Hayes, a nutritional neuroscientist at the University of Pennsylvania, who has studied GLP-1 and other gut hormones since 2006, explains that these drugs work partly because they slow digestion and modulate glucose levels. Some metabolic effect is causing weight loss, but it's "only contributing to a small degree," he says. "The way in which GLP-1 drugs are causing weight loss is without question due to suppression of food intake–to satiety," Hayes adds. Increased satiety means people eat smaller, less frequent meals.

Scientists have known for some time that GLP-1 seems to have a secondary function as a satiety signal–a ping to the brain to stop eating. In 1996 researchers injected GLP-1 directly into the brains of hungry rats, and the rodents' food intake decreased by as much as 95 percent. The study was some of the first evidence that the hormone had an effect in the brain. "All these feelings we have about being hungry or full are fundamentally brain-driven," explains Herman Pontzer, an evolutionary anthropologist at Duke University and author of *Burn*, a book about the science of metabolism. "It makes sense that that's where the mechanism of action is." The brain was always involved, he says, but these new drugs are helping researchers zero in on the brain as a "center for regulating energy in and energy out."

Appetite–the drive to eat–is biologically motivated by three core sensations: hunger, fullness and reward. "All three speak to each other, and for that, parts of the brain play a role," explains Giles Yeo, a University of Cambridge professor who specializes in the genetics of body weight and the neuroscience of food intake. The hypothalamus–an almond-shaped structure near the base of the brain–is involved with feelings of hunger or starvation; the hindbrain, including regions of the brain stem, plays a role in fullness; and a distributed network fanning out from the midbrain to the prefrontal cortex orchestrates reward elements. It produces "the nice feeling you feel from eating chocolate that you don't get from eating broccoli," Yeo explains.

These brain regions all sense signals communicated via the gut-brain axis network–and scientists have found they are studded with GLP-1 receptors. "The receptor-expressing cells are everywhere, *everywhere*, throughout the brain," Hayes says. "It's almost a question of where are they *not*?" In fact, these receptors are now known to be abundant throughout the body. He thinks the reason so many cells and neurons are making GLP-1 receptors must be "because they want to respond to it."

When GLP-1 released from the gut latches on to the vagus nerve, the nerve sends signals up the brain stem to the nucleus tractus solitarius (NTS), a bundle of sensory neurons deep in the brain. The NTS is "the first place that [receives] all incoming satiety signaling from the gut," Hayes says. "It's like a processing hub for energy-balance control."

Because of its short lifespan, it's unlikely that natural GLP-1 produced in the intestines reaches high enough concentrations in the brain to affect satiety. But the NTS doesn't just relay incoming satiety signals from the gut–it also produces GLP-1 itself. Although the details of the mechanism are not yet fully understood, researchers have found that the primary source of GLP-1 in the brain is preproglucagon (PPG) neurons in the NTS. When activated, they act like an emergency brake at the end of the meal, flooding the brain with GLP-1 to send the message to stop eating. This effectively shuts down areas in the brain involved in feeding response, homeostatic controls, energy balance and decision-making about food–as well as the liking and wanting of food and impulsive behaviors associated with eating. For people with obesity, these neurons and hormonal activity might be a clue–one that the new drugs are bringing to light.

Compared with the naturally occurring hormone, the drugs have a stronger structure that better withstands degradation and allows them to be bioactive for hours–the newest formulas can last up to a week. This gives them the potential to act on the brain and stimulate those receptors for longer periods, Mojsov says.

There's growing evidence in animal models that the drugs make it through the blood-brain barrier–a protective membrane surrounding most of the organ–by penetrating "leaky" areas, such as the NTS. One way they get in is by riding on tanycytes, cells that aid in communicating energy balance between the peripheral and central nervous systems and enable nutrients, hormones and drugs to cross the blood-brain barrier.

"What's interesting with these GLP-1-based drugs is that they're lasting a lot longer than [natural] GLP-1," Kanoski says. "This opens up a whole new pathway for communication." Hayes says researchers are now looking into how much GLP-1 gets in, where exactly the drugs go, and what behaviors or functions they cause. "How deep into the brain do they get?" Hayes asks.

"My whole life was thinking about food," says Meranda Hall, a 33-year-old administrator at a law firm in New York City. Hall was a cross-country runner in high school, and she kept exercising daily into adulthood. But she ate almost constantly and had been carrying extra weight since childhood. Even when Hall felt physically full, her brain was occupied by thoughts of food. "While I was eating," she says, "I'd be thinking about the next meal."

In August 2023, when Hall began taking Wegovy, she weighed 271 pounds. Nine months later she'd lost 78 pounds–as well as her intrusive thoughts about eating. The vanishing compulsion to overindulge didn't stop with food, though. Hall says she used to be an enthusiastic social drinker, "an eight-margs-at-Taco-Tuesday type of girl." Now she's "a sober Sally."

Like Hall, some people using GLP-1 receptor agonists report not only a decreased desire for food but reduced cravings for alcohol, nicotine, drugs, online shopping, nail picking–the list goes on. These effects are driving a spate of research into possible overlapping circuitry linking compulsive behaviors, appetite and satiety.

Neurons that produce dopamine–a chemical with pivotal involvement in motivation and pleasure–project to the nucleus accumbens, a midbrain structure important for experiencing reward, explains Patricia "Sue" Grigson, a neuroscientist and addiction researcher at Penn State College of Medicine. Like other brain structures, the nucleus accumbens has GLP-1 receptors. Studies have shown that in animals, dopamine release peaks after they eat a sweet meal of sucrose–and after they are exposed to cocaine or opioids. "But when there's a GLP-1 agonist onboard, that's pretty much squelched," Grigson says. "You don't get a peak to those rewards."

In human experiments, scientists have observed that the same neurological pathways are stimulated when people gamble or take cocaine–or when their blood sugar levels have been artificially changed to stimulate fasting. Janice Jin Hwang, chief of the division of endocrinology and metabolism at the University of North Carolina at Chapel Hill, explains that "there are these networks of brain regions that have been very well characterized, mainly in addiction literature, that control our desire and motivation for food but also for addicting things."

One reason food lights up reward pathways is that it's essential for survival, says Lorenzo Leggio, an addiction researcher at the National Institute on Alcohol Abuse and Alcoholism and the National Institute on Drug Abuse. Visuals, taste, smell, memory, and other cues work together to reinforce food-seeking behavior, and "GLP-1 is trying to keep that process somehow under control," Leggio says. "You start eating your cake. You love it, but what is preventing you from eating, like, 20 pieces of cake? GLP-1 is one of the triggers that is increasing your satiety," he explains. "It's reducing your reward, your pleasure, for that cake."

Grigson and Leggio are among a growing number of researchers studying the effects of GLP-1 medications on this reward pathway for potential addiction treatments. In a clinical trial, Grigon and her colleagues tested the safety and efficacy of daily injections of a GLP-1 receptor agonist, liraglutide, in people receiving treatment for opioid use disorder. They saw an approximately 40 percent reduction in opioid cravings. (Full results are not yet published.)

Grigson's team found that administering GLP-1 drugs in combination with buprenorphine, a current treatment for opioid use disorder, was also highly effective. Buprenorphine is an opioid itself, and people taking it as a medication may continue to experience drug cravings. Grigson hopes that adding GLP-1 medicines might help reduce the amount of buprenorphine needed. She is currently conducting a multisite follow-up study with researchers at New York University to investigate the treatment's effects on withdrawal. In May 2024 Novo Nordisk announced that an upcoming clinical trial would investigate GLP-1 drugs as a treatment for liver disease–and explore their effects on alcohol consumption.

Endocrinologist Ania Jastreboff tells her patients that GLP-1 medications may change their desire to eat. But not everyone experiences the same dramatic effects. "I kind of preface by saying we don't know who will respond and how they will respond, how much weight a certain individual may lose, and how that may also impact their health overall," says Jastreboff, who is director of Yale University's Obesity Research Center. Some people on semaglutide have lost as much as 20 percent of their body weight. But in one study, nearly 18 percent of users lost less than 5 percent. Some people are unable to tolerate the drugs because of their side effects, particularly severe nausea and diarrhea–a 2021 study showed 4.5 percent of people taking semaglutide discontinued the drug because of gastrointestinal issues. Scientists are now seeking to understand why the efficacy seems to vary so dramatically.

Natural GLP-1 levels may differ from person to person, and that could possibly explain varying susceptibility to weight gain or diabetes. Yeo studies why some people eat too much and says maybe it's because they "feel less full for every given mouthful of food they eat. And part of that could be because their GLP-1 levels don't go up as high for a given meal." In those people, Yeo says, synthetic GLP-1 drugs may work better than they would in people with naturally higher levels.

Hayes wonders whether people who aren't responsive to the drugs might have mutations in their GLP-1 receptors—and whether that could be part of why they gained excess weight in the first place. He speculates that GLP-1 receptors in some people may have genetic differences that might influence how well the hormone binds to the receptor and activates subsequent insulin and satiety pathways.

Pharmaceutical companies are creating even more potent weight-loss medications by targeting multiple gut hormone receptors at once. Eli Lilly's tirzepatide uses synthetic versions of GLP-1 and gastric inhibitory polypeptide; clinical trials revealed it caused people to lose more than 25 percent of their body weight over 88 weeks.

The U.S. clinical trial registry shows that thousands of studies on GLP-1 receptor agonists are underway now. A large, multiyear study that showed semaglutide reduced risk of heart attack and stroke by 20 percent helped Wegovy gain FDA approval as a treatment for cardiovascular disease in March 2024. Weight reduction most likely played a large role in heart health, but researchers are also finding convincing early evidence that GLP-1—and the drugs—may reduce inflammation when bound to receptors. That observation is now opening up the drugs to clinical trials for diseases that seem less obviously related to metabolic disorders, including Alzheimer's, Parkinson's, depression and even cancer.

As new findings emerge, GLP-1 medications are changing how researchers and clinicians think about body weight. Health issues that manifest as diabetes or obesity have been primarily considered peripheral disorders—problems of the pancreas, liver or body tissue—Hwang says, but this is only part of the picture. Jastreboff, who has been working on obesity treatments for 15 years, says the drugs are probes to better understand the physiology of obesity. "They've enabled us to have a conversation about obesity as a complex neurometabolic disease," she says.

For so long people who couldn't lose weight and keep it off have been told that their willpower simply wasn't strong enough, says Daniel Drucker, an endocrinologist at the University of Toronto, who researched GLP-1 alongside Mojsov in the 1990s. "We—including health-care professionals–would blame people challenged by their inability to lose weight," he says. "It's hard to think of diseases where we blame the individual. You would never say, 'Your cancer came back; you didn't really try hard enough.'" The study of GLP-1 could help erode the stigma associated with obesity and addiction by replacing assumptions with clear pathology.

"We all have the same reward systems that are absolutely essential to normal functioning," Pontzer says, "and it's only when we get toward the real far end of the spectrum on those reward responses that we get into trouble." This hormonal system is evolutionarily ancient. "And we are now, in 2024, finding the advantages of the system through these drugs–we have hijacked it, if you will," Hayes says. "We are at the precipice of the beginning."

About the Author

Lauren J. Young is an associate editor for health and medicine at Scientific American. *She has edited and written stories that tackle a wide range of subjects, including the COVID pandemic, emerging diseases, evolutionary biology and health inequities. Young has nearly a decade of newsroom and science journalism experience. Before joining* Scientific American *in 2023, she was an associate editor at* Popular Science *and a digital producer at public radio's* Science Friday. *She has appeared as a guest on radio shows, podcasts and stage events. Young has also spoken on panels for the Asian American Journalists Association, American Library Association, NOVA Science Studio and the New York Botanical Garden. Her work has appeared in* Scholastic MATH, School Library Journal, IEEE Spectrum, Atlas Obscura *and* Smithsonian Magazine. *Young studied biology at California Polytechnic State University, San Luis Obispo, before pursuing a master's at New York University's Science, Health & Environmental Reporting Program.*

Section 4: Technology on the Menu

Florida's Beef with Lab-Grown Meat Is Evidence-Free

By Allison Parshall

This week Florida's governor Ron DeSantis signed a bill banning the production and sale of lab-grown meat, also called cultured meat, in the state.

"Florida is fighting back against the global elite's plan to force the world to eat meat grown in a petri dish or bugs to achieve their authoritarian goals," DeSantis said in a statement on Wednesday. "We will save our beef."

There is, however, no indication the U.S. beef market is under threat–from cultured meat, bugs or otherwise. Red meat production and consumption are holding steady overall in the country. In contrast, cultured meat, which is grown from small numbers of real animal cells and does not require any killing, only received its first regulatory approvals in the U.S. last year and isn't available for consumers to buy yet.

"No one in the field has yet scaled up to the levels you need to produce food for supermarkets," says David Kaplan, a biomolecular engineer focusing on cellular agriculture at Tufts University. "There's not even an industry yet. It's just fledgling!"

But Florida's legislature has stepped in–purportedly to prevent the cultured meat industry from competing with traditional agriculture. Alabama, Arizona and Tennessee may soon follow suit. Cultured meat's detractors use words like "franken-meat," "petri dishes" and "chemicals" in an apparent attempt to evoke disgust. Yet this emotional rhetoric is not founded in the reality of cultured meat production, which has already been approved for certain companies by two regulatory agencies and has the potential to be safer to consume than traditionally farmed meats, experts say.

Cultured meat starts as a small number of muscle and fat cells in samples taken from living animals. These cells are placed in giant vats that contain a broth of nutrients and hormones that encourage the cells to grow and divide. Companies developing cultured meat will sometimes compare these vats to what you'd find at a brewery.

To make products that look less like ground meat and more like a chicken breast or cut of salmon, developers will sometimes imbue their creations with edible "scaffolds" that give the cells a more structured texture and appearance. Creating these structured cuts is easier for some meats than others: some companies produce a nice cultured salmon filet, but replicating the marbled texture of a steak is a much greater challenge. "There's a lot of tech development that has to happen," Kaplan notes.

While there's no reason to think cultivated meat will be any more or less nutritious than meat from a traditional farm, it could be safer to consume. "Every step of the process that we use for cultivated meat is highly controlled," Kaplan says. "If there were any contamination [of the meat], we would know it as soon as it happens." That's compared with traditional agricultural methods, which often rely on copious amounts of antibiotics to prevent pathogens such as salmonella from contaminating meat. In principle, a scaled-up version of cultured meat production would require less antibiotic use because it could be so tightly controlled.

"In terms of safety, health, nutrition, we anticipate [cultured meat] will be, at minimum, as safe as current foods—and more likely safer in the long run," Kaplan says.

But many lawmakers and lobbyists who are looking to ban cultured meat are not appealing to rational concerns about health and safety in their rhetoric. Some are instead taking advantage of an emotional response many humans have toward something they perceive as unfamiliar and unnatural, says Matti Wilks, a psychology researcher at the University of Edinburgh, who has studied attitudes toward cultured meat.

"It's easier for people to push back on something like [cultured meat] if it's already something that people feel a bit uncomfortable about," Wilks says. The idea that cultured meat is unnatural comes not from analytic reasoning but from emotional responses such as disgust and fear, she found in a 2020 study. And in a paper published in March, she found that people who have negative opinions of cultured meat are more likely to value purity over other core moral concepts such as not doing harm.

Humans are particularly attuned to feelings of disgust when it comes to food, sex and other things related to the body. And the "bad feeling" some people might get when they think of an unfamiliar kind of food can't always be reasoned away, Wilks says. "That bad feeling ... might be a way to justify that it's unnatural," she adds.

Chris Bryant, a psychologist and director of the U.K.-based company Bryant Research, where he studies attitudes toward cultured meat, encourages people to examine their own knee-jerk feelings of disgust. "The production process for conventional meat is also pretty disgusting, if one cares to look at it," he says. That's especially true for factory-farmed meats, which comprise the vast majority of meats produced in the U.S. "Would you rather have to watch the production process for cultivated meats or have to watch the production process for conventional meat?" he asks. "I think that needs to be the bar for comparison."

The idea that "natural" or unprocessed foods are healthier is deeply ingrained in our culture, but many experts say this is largely based on a very common flaw in reasoning called the naturalistic fallacy.

"This idea that 'processed' means that it's unhealthy as just unscientific," Bryant says. And that's "not only a bit difficult as a nuance to understand, but there are people trying deliberately to get you to misunderstand them."

DeSantis signed the bill at a press conference, where he stood against the backdrop of an idyllic red barn in the presence of members of the Florida Cattlemen's Association. And agriculture lobbying groups have long fought alternatives to animal products that now proliferate supermarket shelves. Kaplan says he sees these attempts as shortsighted.

"It's going to take a while to have any impact" on farmers, Kaplan says. And cultured meat production still requires farmers and livestock for many steps in its production, he notes. "We see so many places where we're going to need farmers," Kaplan adds.

About the Author

Allison Parshall is an associate news editor at Scientific American *who often covers biology, health, technology and physics. She edits the magazine's Contributors column and weekly online Science Quizzes. As a multimedia journalist, Parshall contributes to* Scientific American's *podcast* Science Quickly. *Her work includes a three-part miniseries on music-making artificial intelligence. Her work has also appeared in* Quanta Magazine *and* Inverse. *Parshall graduated from New York University's Arthur L. Carter Journalism Institute with a master's degree in science, health and environmental reporting. She has a bachelor's degree in psychology from Georgetown University. Follow Parshall on X (formerly Twitter) @parshallison*

Tweaking Vegetables' Genes Could Make Them Tastier—And You'll Get to Try Them Soon

By Meghan Bartels

Today's Brussels sprouts taste better than you might remember from childhood. It's not that your refined adult palate appreciates them better. Rather a new variety has displaced the original vegetable. You can thank plant breeders for the change. And modern breeders, armed with new gene-editing technology, are looking to replicate Brussels sprouts' reinvention.

In the late 1990s scientists identified specific chemicals, called glucosinolates, that made Brussels sprouts taste bitter. Plant breeders started growing old seeds, previously discarded for producing paltry harvests, to identify tastier versions with lower levels of these compounds. Then they crossed these delicious but low-yield plants with modern, more prolific individuals until they found a descendant that made plenty of tasty sprouts, transforming the once maligned vegetable from a bitter pill into a popular side dish.

But other veggies haven't fared as well. That's because most breeding decisions favor plant traits that matter to vegetable growers, not vegetable eaters. "I'd say disease resistance is probably the major focus these days of most breeding programs because that's what imperils the ability of the farmer to grow the crop," says Harry Klee, a professor emeritus of horticulture at the University of Florida, who specializes in tomatoes. "Quality traits are really completely ignored."

In addition, breeders who focus on consumer crops must navigate the controversy surrounding genetically modified organisms (GMOs). Although all domesticated species now have different genetics than their ancestors, in agriculture, the term GMO refers to a plant that carries genes imported from a completely different species—and these changes are subject to stricter regulation. But newer techniques are allowing breeders to work within the context of a plant's own genome, making tweaks that don't trigger complicated rules.

Flavor is challenging to target because different people have different preferences–plus, even under the best conditions, flavor quality is more complex than something like yield. "We've spent a lot of time and money figuring out what flavor is, and most breeding programs don't have the capacity to measure those things," Klee says.

But interest in prioritizing flavor is starting to build, thanks in part to new genetic technology such as the gene-snipping technique CRISPR and DNA sequencing that is cheap enough to use liberally. "There's never been a better time to be a fruit breeder or a vegetable breeder because we have more tools and techniques," says Susan Brown, an apple breeder at Cornell University.

Some companies are beginning to use those tools to tackle the challenge of developing tastier veggies. One company, Pairwise, is fighting the same compounds that plagued Brussels sprouts: glucosinolates. But this time researchers are modifying salad greens–and they're armed with the science of gene editing.

Although kale, for instance, is particularly healthy, many prefer eating the less bitter romaine or iceberg lettuce. So Pairwise scientists figured out how to use CRISPR to edit a kalelike mustard green to fit that palate. They wanted to turn off the genes that code for an enzyme called myrosinase, which breaks down the glucosinolates and creates bitterness once the leaf is chewed in a diner's mouth. The result is a healthy but less bitter green that the company is marketing this year under the brand Conscious Foods.

This is an example of where flavor-minded gene editing can shine, says Tom Adams, co-founder and CEO of Pairwise. "From a gene-editing perspective, I think where taste comes in is that we can remove things that people don't like," he says. "It's a lot more difficult to think about how you can bring in the really complex, great tastes." To create those more complex tastes, Adams says, traditional breeding is still the best path.

Traditional breeding is the cornerstone of another high-tech flavor effort as well, one that seeks to reverse the ways of thinking that got us to tasteless vegetables in the first place. Instead of growing varieties that can withstand the storage and transportation needs of the agricultural system, a company called Plenty is shrinking the vast distance from the field to the table. Plenty grows its plants in indoor vertical farming facilities closer to consumers, so produce stays fresher, says Nate Storey, the company's co-founder and chief science officer.

When Plenty decided to start with greens, he says, the team grew thousands of traditionally bred varieties in its facilities. Then the researchers adopted only the ones that resulted in the tastiest crops rather than trying to develop new varieties. "There's no need to rebuild a wheel," Storey says of the technique. "We just screen all the wheels that exist and find the ones that work best in our system."

This method does not always succeed, however. The company couldn't find a tomato that thrived in its facilities, so it's working on developing its own variety using a sped-up version of traditional breeding.

Tomatoes are a popular target. A third company is creating more flavorful tomatoes using epigenetics–changing the expression of genes instead of the genes themselves. Whereas Pairwise is snipping out the gene sequences that produce an enzyme that interferes with flavor, Sound Agriculture is programming gene expression. This approach dials down production of undesirable compounds by making their genetic sequences less accessible for transcription.

Understanding how precisely to modify expression to get a desired result is still a work in progress, says Travis Bayer, co-founder and chief technology officer of Sound Agriculture. "The science of epigenetics in plants is really exciting and it's something that is evolving pretty rapidly," he says. The company's first epigenetically grown product, a tomato dubbed Summer Swell, is due to hit shelves this spring. Other projects in the works focus on leafy greens, as well as a handful of fruits, Bayer says.

All these vegetable growers hope that more flavorful products on store shelves will convince people to consume the recommended allowances of fruits and vegetables—and do so better than decades of nutritional guidance have.

"Don't waste your time talking about trying to educate people to eat better," says Klee, the tomato breeding researcher. "Just give them products that taste better, that they want to eat."

About the Author

Meghan Bartels is a science journalist based in New York City. She joined Scientific American *in 2023 and is now a senior news reporter there. Previously, she spent more than four years as a writer and editor at Space.com, as well as nearly a year as a science reporter at* Newsweek, *where she focused on space and Earth science. Her writing has also appeared in* Audubon, Nautilus, Astronomy *and* Smithsonian, *among other publications. She attended Georgetown University and earned a master's degree in journalism at New York University's Science, Health and Environmental Reporting Program.*

Robotic Bees Could Support Vertical Farms Today and Astronauts Tomorrow

By Molly Glick

In vertical farming operations, artificial lights and artificial intelligence coax plants, stacked densely on towering shelves rather than spread over a field, to grow indoors with minimal human intervention. That's the goal. But despite lofty promises of bringing fresh produce to local markets, these systems have not yet provided a climate-friendly way to feed the world's growing population. Can robotic "bees," a buzzy technology straight out of science fiction, rescue these high-tech operations?

The world's first commercial vertical farm opened in Singapore in 2012. More businesses cropped up in the following years, with major players such as Infarm and AeroFarms securing hundreds of millions in funding over the next decade. With the help of sustainable systems such as hydroponics, as well as artificial intelligence to closely monitor plant growth and water usage, some companies and experts claim these futuristic farms could tackle global food insecurity–without the massive land and water footprint of conventional operations.

These farms "have the potential to contribute a meaningful amount to our diets," says Thomas Graham, who researches controlled environment agriculture at the University of Guelph in Ontario. And companies can place them nearly anywhere.

Many vertical farms' hopes have dried up over the past year, however. Recent inflation and worldwide skyrocketing energy prices, fueled by Russia's invasion of Ukraine, rendered these farms' near-constant electricity demand unaffordable. This past fall Infarm announced it was laying off more than half of its employees, and AeroFarms recently filed for bankruptcy. Meanwhile other vertical farm ventures are also facing financial challenges.

It doesn't help that vertical farms currently have a limited range of offerings; most grow only greens such as lettuce and herbs because they use low amounts of water and are relatively easy to cultivate indoors via hydroponics thanks to their speedy development. "Some of the work we're doing is moving past just leafy greens," Graham says. "You can't feed the world on lettuce."

To truly take on food insecurity, vertical farms must expand their offerings, and that means finding a way to bring pollinators into high-tech indoor farming operations. Around one third of the crops we eat require pollinators such as bees and bats to grow. It's difficult to get the job done in a vertical farm because domesticated honeybees, one of the most popular pollinators forcommercial growers, have trouble navigating under artificial light, and pollinating by hand is extremely time intensive and thus expensive. To solve the problem, researchers have been working on robotic pollinators for more than a decade. But such pollinators have only recently made their way to universities and commercial operations.

Bee Bots to the Rescue

Bots aren't new to farms. Since the mid-20th century researchers have explored ways to automate agriculture, including tractors with automated steering. By the 1980s and 1990s, engineers had begun tinkering with task-specific devices such as a robotic melon harvester and tomato-picking robots. Companies are now developing autonomous bots to harvest a variety of produce, and some devices can also accomplish additional tasks, including weeding, pesticide spraying and disease monitoring. Artificial intelligence helps most of these tools organize and process information from their onboard sensors—often multispectral cameras, which can pick up on differences in the types of light reflected by plants. Those differences provide clues about a crop's health, such as ripeness in fruit or signs of damage.

Although most agricultural-machine research still focuses on produce-picking bots, more teams are now aiming to automate pollination as well, says Mahla Nejati, a research fellow at the University of Auckland in New Zealand, who works on farming-oriented robotics and AI systems. For her Ph.D. project, Nejati developed the computer vision system for an autonomous kiwi- and apple-picking bot designed for orchards. Eventually, her colleagues had a revelation: because they were already picking robotically, it would have been "better to have started earlier with the pollination," Nejati says.

Now scientists and businesses around the world are grappling with the best ways to design and implement robo pollinators. This is not a simple task, says Yu Gu, a roboticist at West Virginia University, who is developing a six-armed pollinating machine called the StickBug. To build widely useable pollinators, "I think it's a big problem that there's so many types of flowers and so many types of agriculture settings," he says.

Some researchers have carried their work outside of academia and into the market. Siddharth Jadhav, who previously studied drone aerodynamics at the National University of Singapore, founded a company called Polybee in 2019. He and his colleagues adapt widely available mini drones for various types of indoor agriculture operations, including vertical farms and greenhouses. Polybee's AI-powered software instructs drones equipped with color camera sensors that measure key traits for growers to fly near plants. Then the drones carefully disturb the air around them to vibrate flowers when the conditions inside greenhouses (such as temperature and humidity) are optimal for pollination, Jadhav says. This activity shakes the pollen out of the flower and kicks off the fertilization process.

Polybee currently sells its pollination system to commercial tomato greenhouses in Australia. (Compared with many other food crops, tomato pollination is relatively straightforward because the plants' flowers have both male and female parts.) The team has also run trials with indoor vertical farming companies, Jadhav says, although "we do not have many commercial vertical farms that grow fruit crops at scale yet."

An Israel-based company called Arugga also sells bots to tomato greenhouses. Its roving ground robot, aptly named Polly, moves between rows of plants and blasts pulses of air to prompt pollination. The process is mostly autonomous. For now, however, human operators must move Polly between rows by operating a tablet. Arugga may eventually delve into vertical farming but only if that market becomes more profitable, says Eytan Heller, the company's co-founder and vice president of business development.

Still, if robotic pollinators do pan out for vertical farms, they could offer multiple advantages. For one, they could reduce infections between plants because bees can spread diseases that cause major damage to farms. For more than two decades, scientists around the world have suggested that bumblebees can spread viruses to previously uninfected tomatoes that can render them unsellable. Commercially developed bees deployed in greenhouses can also slip outside and infect wild bees nearby, which are already experiencing a rapid decline that is largely linked to factors such as climate change, urbanization and pesticide use. This is especially damaging for the plants that rely on those outdoor pollinators because they can't fall back on their own mechanical substitutes. According to Nejati, bots perform best indoors, where they can move around highly structured environments and avoid unpredictable weather and temperatures.

What's Next for Robo Bees

While Polybee and Arugga claim they've got the tomato pollination game down pat, they're still working on modifying their products to work with other types of plants. Polybee is currently running trials with strawberries, and Arugga says its tools can be adjusted to work with plenty of other crops, such as strawberries and blueberries.

But each plant comes with its own complexities, Gu says. While Arugga plans to use its pulsing-air method for various types of fruit, Gu and his colleagues have found that certain varieties may require direct contact with robots, similar to the natural method performed by bees. After collaborating with a range of experts, including entomologists and horticulturalists, he thinks that some types of berries, for example, likely benefit from contact-based pollination. Graham agrees that certain berries probably would benefit from direct interactions with robots, perhaps small drones.

Regardless of the fruit, bots will have to work gently to avoid damaging flowers, which tend to be delicate. Gu compares the pollination process to "robotic surgery" and says that, for now, the drone airflow method will likely be limited to working with several plants at once rather than individuals. "The crop that needs precision pollination [is] disturbed by the airflow," he says. "It's difficult to operate that precisely."

Even if robotic pollinators rescue vertical farms from obsolescence, it's unlikely that any type of indoor agriculture can entirely replace the fields humans have relied on for millennia. But he suggests that vertical farms could supplement outdoor crops without taking up too much space. For instance, they can be built on abandoned pieces of land. "This is a complementary way of doing things," Graham says. "We need to rethink agriculture in the face of climate change and population growth, but [vertical farms] shouldn't be looked at as competitive–because they're not."

Vertical farms could additionally aid another location that's short on natural resources: outer space. Graham, who also researches food production on the final frontier, says robotic pollinators could be particularly helpful in this environment. While scientists already plan to bring living insects to space to work as pollinators and to eat waste, the insects' metal counterparts would likely live longer. ("Worker" bumblebees only survive for a few weeks.) Astronauts could even 3-D-print these tools off-planet.

"Space is a neat field because nothing is really off the table," he says. "It's all under consideration, and ultimately–like most things–[space farming will] probably be some sort of hybrid."

About the Author

Molly Glick is a freelance science journalist based in New York City. Their writing has appeared in Inverse, Discover, Popular Science *and other publications. You can follow them on Twitter @mollyglick and read more of their work on their website.*

Why Is It So Hard to Make Vegan Fish?

By Joanna Thompson

When I went vegetarian a decade ago, I found it pretty painless to pass on most animal-based dishes. Burgers? Plant-based patties were abundant and, for the most part, delicious. Poultry? Easy: vegan chicken nuggets tasted just like the real deal. Pork? I'd never been a huge fan in the first place. My one weakness was sushi. No matter where I looked, I just couldn't find a satisfying veggie alternative to my favorite form of seafood.

It's only now, 10 years later, that new food science innovations could finally make the vegan, whole-cut fish of my dreams a reality. This year several alternative protein companies are launching or already offering their first crop of plant-based filets, promising to replicate the taste and texture of real fish. But why is it so hard to make a good piece of vegan salmon in the first place?

It turns out that flavor is the easy part. The rather specific taste common to fresh fish comes mostly from a combination of molecules that scientists already know how to replicate in a lab: long-chain fatty acids, such as omega-3s and omega-6s, which give fish their oily quality and taste, and volatile carbonyls, which lend a lighter, almost melonlike flavor. The real challenge of vegan fish is nailing the mouthfeel. "When the texture is enjoyable, you can take the dish in many directions," says Guy Vaknin, a chef who heads four vegan restaurants in New York City, including Beyond Sushi. "It's a great canvas."

"Fish has a very special texture," says Atze Jan van der Goot, a food process engineer at Wageningen University & Research in the Netherlands. Most cuts of fish actually contain several layers of short-fiber muscle, which are held together with thin bands of connective tissue and fat. Within each layer, bundles of microscopic muscle fibers are arranged like the teeth of a comb, all pointing in the same direction. It's this structure that gives cooked fish its unique flaky quality.

But most processes for making meat substitutes aren't designed to mimic muscle fiber. Instead they aim for a far simpler consistency: that of ground meat, which can be pressed into burger patty, sausage or nugget form. "I think a lot of meat is consumed via nugget-type products," van der Goot says, "especially in the U.S."

The food-processing technique that best achieves nugget texture in vegetarian meat substitutes is called extrusion. It involves grinding raw food material, such as grains, vegetable proteins and various additives, into fine particles and then forcing the resulting "dough" through a tube under high pressure. As it squeezes through this opening, the food slurry is cooked simultaneously by added steam and the heat of its own friction.

Like the *Star Trek* "replicator," extruders can squirt out an astronomical range of prepackaged edibles–everything from Cheerios to cheese puffs to chewing gum relies on this process. The catch is that such products all have a similar texture, and they can't be extruded raw. The process generates so much heat that it denatures, or unravels, most of the available protein molecules in the extruded material, rendering it somewhat shapeless. This is perfectly fine if people want to purchase a vegan crab cake. But it presents a challenge if they're shopping for a raw fish substitute in order to re-create the experience of, say, biting into uncooked salmon crudo or searing a juicy tuna steak.

Luckily, food scientists are now finding creative new ways to re-create fish's intricate sheets of parallel muscle fiber. One such technique is called directional freezing. This process capitalizes on the fact that ice tends to form in a certain direction–starting from the coldest point and moving outward. It also tends to adhere to itself, freezing in pure crystals of H_2O. Some food researchers have applied directional freezing to blocks of gel made from edible algae. As the gel freezes, the water inside it solidifies into needlelike ice structures, creating a matrix of thousands of tiny tubes. This perforated gel makes a great scaffolding for uncooked faux fish.

That's the strategy that New School Foods, a Canadian alternative meat start-up, is using to craft its plant-based raw salmon and tuna filets. "It's basically like a directional sponge," says Auke de Vries, New School Foods' lead food materials scientist. Adjusting the size of the gel matrix or tweaking its freezing temperature can yield differently sized or shaped channels, "which is important because that's the main driver of texture," de Vries says.

Once the scaffolding is in place, the food science researchers can fill the channels by injecting them with whatever mixture of protein, fat and flavor they want. The options include 100 percent plant-based proteins, such as soy, pea or gluten, and–potentially–actual animal cells cultured in the lab. They can also add volatile flavor compounds that might otherwise break down in a precooked product. "We're not married to any one ingredient," says New School Foods founder Chris Bryson.

But there's more than one way to skin a vegan catfish. Another method gaining traction in the alternative seafood world is 3-D printing. Revo Foods, a plant-based seafood manufacturer in Vienna, uses 3-D food printers to build smoked salmon filets from the ground up with carefully constructed layers of pea protein, algal extracts and omega-3 fatty acids.

If all of these techniques sound elaborate, it's because they are. But the technology to make vegan meat and seafood is getting cheaper by the day, and its proponents believe the environmental benefits far outweigh the production hassle. "The impact that overfishing and harmful fishing practices have on vulnerable ocean ecosystems is very serious," says Birgit Dekkers, a food scientist and co-founder of the Dutch plant based meat company Rival Foods.

According to the Food and Agriculture Organization of the United Nations, overfishing and habitat destruction have depleted more than one third of global fish stocks. Not only does this wreak havoc on aquatic ecosystems, it can even contribute to global climate change by reducing the number of species available to store carbon.

"The overall carbon footprint of ocean trawling is equivalent to the carbon footprint of the entire aviation industry," Bryson says.

Persuading more people to switch to sustainable plant-based seafood isn't going to fix climate change. But it could be a step toward ensuring that there are always plenty of fish in the sea.

About the Author

Joanna Thompson is an insect enthusiast and former Scientific American *intern. She is based in New York City. Follow Thompson on Twitter @jojofoshosho0*

Flavor-Enhancing Spoons and Chopsticks Could Make Food Taste Better

By Saugat Bolakhe

Foods high in sugar and salt can be unhealthy, but these additives are too delicious for many to give up. What if people could somehow enjoy these compounds' tastes without actually eating them? A student team has now designed a spoon with a structure that stimulates taste buds to produce a sensation of sweetness—without adding calories or chemicals. The project follows previous work involving flavor-enhancing cutlery, such as chopsticks that amplify saltiness with a mild electric current.

The five undergraduate and graduate research students wanted to develop their new spoon for people with disorders such as diabetes, which affects 11.3 percent of the U.S. population. Many with this condition have to limit their sugar intake.

The spoon, called Sugarware, would have several bumps on its underside, creating a greater surface area to press against the tongue, and its surface would be coated with a permanent layer of molecules called ligands. These ligands bind with cell-surface receptor proteins that typically react to sugar molecules or artificial sweeteners, triggering a cascade of nerve signals that cause the brain to register a sensation of sweetness. A diner could thus "stimulate sweetness receptors ... without actual injection of sugar or artificial sweeteners," the team explained during the 2022 Biodesign Sprint, an online educational competition. Sugarware won its designers the runner up spot in the student category.

The researchers cite two influences for Sugarware. "We got our design inspirations from a Korean designer, Jinhyun Jeon," says Shiyu Xu, who was a graduate researcher in animal science at Cornell University when the project was developed. Jeon's work on synesthesia has explored how the senses can affect one another while eating. In one project, "she was using a similar kind of knobby spoon to experiment [with] how the eating experience can change and can get affected by those spoons," says team member Weiran Tao, a graduate telecommunications researcher at New York University.

Research by Jeon and others focuses on how textures influence taste perception, sometimes in unlikely and intriguing ways. For a past project, University of Oxford experimental psychologist Charles Spence, who is not involved in the Sugarware project, found that people who consumed ginger cookies, coffee or wine while rubbing sandpaper with their fingers rated the taste differently than when they rubbed a smooth surface. Spence says he is not sure about the reason, but "maybe the roughness of sandpaper matches with the pungency of ginger biscuits or the roughness in the mouth of black coffee." Or, in the case of the new spoon, he suggests that "if the texture feels different from what you're used to, then suddenly you sit up and take notice," and that changes the experience.

Xu says the Sugarware team also looked at a Japanese study, by Homei Miyashita of Meiji University and his colleagues, that found ways to stimulate salt receptors in the tongue. With the company Kirin Holdings, Miyashita's group developed specialized chopsticks: a weak electric current runs through this novel cutlery, shifting the sodium ions in a mouthful of food to excite the tongue's salt receptors. The researchers reported that their chopsticks could increase diners' perception of salt by up to one and half times. A U.S. company, Taste Boosters, took a similar microcurrent-based approach with a utensil called SpoonTEK.

These ideas are similar to Sugarware in that they all use utensils to enhance taste without a user having to actually consume any salt or sugar. "But the mechanism for stimulating the taste buds is completely different in Sugarware," Xu says: it uses texture and taste-bud-stimulating molecules rather than electricity.

The Sugarware researchers are also interested in reducing the need for artificial sweeteners. These compounds are integrated into many foods and "consumed by hundreds of millions worldwide with the notion that they generate the sweetest sensation without having the caloric price," says Eran Elinav, a microbiome researcher at

Israel's Weizmann Institute of Science, who is not involved with the student project. But these chemicals do have an effect on the body. In 2014 Elinav's team gave mice the artificial sweetener saccharin and found that the rodents' gut microbiome interacted with the sweetener, affecting the animals' regulation of glucose levels. Other research has demonstrated that humans who consume some sugar substitutes also experience changes in the gut microbiome, as well as spikes in blood glucose. "Artificial sweeteners are clearly not inert in the human body," Elinav says. Because Sugarware would stimulate a sweetness reaction without requiring users to consume anything, it might be able to sidestep this type of interaction.

The idea is "very creative," says one of the Biodesign Sprint judges, Paola de Almeida, who is global director of corporate innovation at candymaker Mars. But the product's commercial success would require a significant behavioral shift among consumers: instead of adding the usual sugar or artificial sweeteners, "now we're saying, 'Use this utensil,'" de Almeida says.

It remains to be seen whether flavor-enhancing utensils will catch on. The Japanese team does not plan to commercialize its electric chopsticks until later this year, and the Sugarware researchers are still working on a prototype. Part of their contest prize includes a mentorship from Mars staff.

But if you want to play around with cutlery and flavor right now, you don't need specially designed forks or knives. Previous research shows that the weight, color and shape of normal utensils can change how people perceive food's taste. So grab a variety of cutlery and hold an independent taste test. You may find some spoons are sweeter than others, even if they're bump-free.

About the Author

Saugat Bolakhe is a freelance science journalist. He studied zoology as an undergraduate in Nepal and received a master's degree from the Craig Newmark Graduate School of Journalism at the City University of New York. His work has appeared in Scientific American, Nature, New Scientist, Quanta, Eos, Discover, Knowable *and other publications.*

Plants Have Hormones, Too, and Tweaking Them Could Improve Food Supply

By Sara Reardon

Between crop damage caused by climate change and a rising global population and nutritional demand, it is clear the world will need to produce more food in the future. Researchers have long studied ways to help plants resist environmental stressors such as pests and drought, both through conventional breeding and genetic modification. But many questions still remain about how, exactly, plants interact with their environment and how scientists might be able to modify those processes to help them adapt.

Researchers at the Institute of Network Biology in Germany and their colleagues may have found a way to help. In early July they published a study in *Nature* showing that plants communicate with the environment in more complex ways than previously thought. The investigation revealed that the information-processing network, driven by hormones, in one genus of plants is carried out by more than 2,000 protein interactions, hundreds of which had not been discovered before. "We're going to need a second green revolution," says Shelley Lumba, a plant biologist at the University of Toronto, who was not involved in the study. "These would be good leads to test."

Unlike animals, which complete most of their development in utero, plants remain relatively flexible throughout their life. Sensory proteins detect changing environmental conditions and then use hormones to cause it to alter its behavior or physiology accordingly. Many pathways are well understood: the hormone ABA, for instance, tells plants to close their pores and conserve water during drought by directing a series of specific proteins to carry out cellular functions.

The flexibility of these hormone networks is precisely what has made them so difficult to genetically modify or engineer to cope with changing climates, however. Most genetically modified crops that are on the market are made by adding a gene from bacteria to a plant's genome—allowing it to resist an herbicide or insecticide, for example. And although the alternative, manipulating proteins, is relatively easy with new genome-editing techniques, "you usually mess up the plants," says Eilon Shani, a plant biologist at Tel Aviv University.

To create crops that resist environmental stressors, researchers have relied on conventional breeding techniques using the genetic diversity that exists naturally among them. They have done so to develop varieties of wheat that produce high levels of ABA, for instance. That sort of breeding has become increasingly difficult in recent years, says Matthew Hudson, a crop scientist at the University of Illinois at Urbana-Champaign. For one thing, many countries have begun banning the export of seeds that have useful properties in order to conserve them as a natural resource.

New technologies, including CRISPR/Cas9 genome editing, can make genetic modification relatively straightforward. Scientists hoping to tweak plant genes must first know what they are looking for, however. Focusing on systems rather than individual genes could prove useful. To activate their defenses against insects, for example, plants might have to shut down another hormone pathway, such as growth or water conservation.

"There are a lot of trade-offs that are fundamental to plant physiology, and we know they're there, but they're not characterized in a quantitative way," Hudson says. Research such as the *Nature* study, he says, could help scientists develop computational models that would reveal how to understand and tweak the pathways through genetic engineering. "This is obviously the next generation of research," Hudson says.

Making plants more flexible might be more important than giving them specific traits. "Hormones permit responses to take place," Lumba says. "They're not instructing; they're allowing environmental stimulation to be read."

Lumba is studying the hormone mechanisms that help certain plants quickly repopulate areas razed by forest fires. When these "fire followers" sense the chemicals emitted from burned materials, they release a hormone called auxin that sparks germination. Yet because all known plants contain auxin, as well as the smoke-sensing proteins, it remains unclear why most of them do not actually respond. Mapping out the extensive pathways between the sensor and the response, she says, could be a step toward helping restore ecosystems after a fire.

Creating crops that quickly adapt to their environments will continue to be a massive endeavor. Most plant researchers studying signaling mechanisms have focused on *Arabidopsis*, a genus of small flowering herbs relatedto cabbage and mustard. A laboratory model of *Arabidopsis* has been extremely well characterized. Revealing the entire network of protein interactions in crops such as corn or rice, Hudson says, would take years and millions of dollars.

Although researchers have been working on genetically modified crop plants that resist drought or other stressors, none of the variations are close to being commercially available. "We have transgenic traits we can add on top [of conventionally bred plants], but we're really not engineering the subtle things that make plants into viable crops," Hudson says. His group and others at the University of Illinois are working on developing computer algorithms to predict how modifying particular genes through engineering would affect a plant's growth. For slow-growing organisms–including walnut trees, which are under threat from a parasitic fungus–such a system could save many years of watching and waiting.

The same advantage is true for noncrop plants. Bingru Huang, a plant biologist at Rutgers University, has genetically modified hormone-signaling pathways in grasses used for golf-course turf and other applications. Increasing the amount of hormones called cytokinins and making the plants more sensitive to their changing levels, she found, made the grasses more resistant to heat and salty soil. Huang says practical genetic engineering of hormone pathways will be difficult, however. "When you change one hormone, others change," she adds.

Ultimately, figuring out the ways plants communicate with their surroundings and adapt to harsh environments could benefit the food supply. “We don’t think we’re smarter than nature and smarter than plants,” Shani says. “But we might help plants adapt faster than waiting another million years for evolution to do its work again.”

About the Author

Sara Reardon is a freelance biomedical journalist based in Bozeman, Mont. She is a former staff reporter at Nature, New Scientist *and* Science *and has a master’s degree in molecular biology.*

Breeding a Nonallergenic Peanut

By Peter Beetham

Peanut butter has been a beloved staple of school lunches for what seems like forever. But peanut *allergy* is a serious condition that can cause fatal reactions when not immediately treated. Peanut allergy afflicts 2–3 percent of children and teenagers in the United States, which amounts to approximately 1.6 million people across the country. Various therapies are under investigation for peanut allergy—including Aimmune's immunotherapy that's being reviewed by the Food and Drug Administration (FDA) – yet these don't target the root problem: the peanut itself.

But what if farmers could grow a peanut that doesn't cause an allergic reaction in the first place?

While researchers have understood the genetics behind the allergy for quite some time, there's been a holdup on developing a peanut that doesn't contain these genes. Plant breeders have lacked the tools needed to make the precise genetic changes required to neutralize the triggers for an allergic response.

Until now.

It's important to understand how peanut allergies came to exist in the first place. Over millennia, genetic changes in peanuts have happened either randomly or been selected by farmers for different breeding techniques. This long and laborious process has meant that certain unfavorable characteristics—such as proteins that trigger life-threatening allergies—have persisted in peanuts and other commercial crops.

But recent advances in gene-editing tools can make changes at the precise place in an organism's DNA that cause these allergic reactions. During an allergic response, the peanuts' storage proteins can trigger a massive overproduction of histamines (chemicals that kick the immune system into overdrive), throwing the body into shock. It's a harmful analogue to what happens when we're frightened and the body produces a flood of adrenaline to turbocharge our system.

Using "molecular scissors" (CRISPRs or TALENs) to knock out the entire genes that produce protein storage won't work, however, because then you wouldn't have a peanut at all. Instead, we need to edit the surface of the protein, so no allergic response is triggered, and we need to do that without changing the function of the genes controlling the storage proteins.

This is a delicate task. If we can envision the relationship between the trigger and the allergic response as a lock and key (respectively), we're trying to change the lock so that the key won't fit. In other words, we're eliminating an undesirable function of a protein while preserving its original structure.

For this, we need a far more precise set of tools than those available in the early years of gene editing. Molecular scissors allow one to eliminate a part or all of a gene, but they don't allow researchers to alter the gene itself. That requires an additional gene editing tool.

Think of a gene as a word constructed out of letters. In genetics, these letters are called nucleotides. A tool known as GRON (Gene Repair OligoNucleotide) functions as a spellchecker that the cell recognizes as a guide to correct its DNA. When guided to the precise letter(s) of DNA involved in triggering the allergic reaction, this guide will harness the plant's own repair mechanisms to change the spelling of the gene so that the key no longer fits the lock, so to speak. The GRON is the technological advance that, in combination with molecular scissors, enables researchers to precisely edit a gene to changes its function without altering it structure.

In some cases, this can be a complex task because the allergic reaction involves more than one gene, and changing the trigger that causes the allergic response requires multiple spelling changes. This can be accomplished only with technology that can edit rather than simply knock out genes. This is why we refer to the combination of the GRON with molecular scissors as "precision gene editing."

However daunting the task of making these spelling changes might be, once accomplished, they will yield benefits far beyond their immediate application to peanut allergy. Nature tends towards efficiency, and a number of the genes and genetic pathways involved in peanut allergy are also involved in other allergies. It also means that in dealing with peanut allergy, we also get a head start in dealing with other plant-related allergic responses ranging from gluten intolerance to reactions to grass.

We have the tools to tackle various allergies, and we know the tools work. The combination of GRON and molecular scissors has already produced a canola that resists plant diseases, as well as crops (including canola, flax and rice) that can tolerate herbicides. By applying this to an allergy-safe peanut, we can foresee a day when parents won't live in fear of allergic exposure when sending their child off to a friend's house for a playdate.

This article was published in Scientific American's former blog network and reflects the views of the author, not necessarily those of Scientific American.

About the Author

Peter Beetham is CEO of CIBUS, an agricultural biotech that specializes in non-transgenic gene editing.

Section 5: The Food Industry's Impact on the Environment

Snake Steak Could Be a Climate-Friendly Source of Protein

By Meghan Bartels

Put aside your chicken cutlets and meatloaf and say hello to python curries and satay skewers. Some snake scientists think eating these reptiles–already customary or at least acceptable in parts of the world–might help lessen the damage our food choices have on the environment.

With some eight billion people on the planet today, all of whom require protein to stay healthy, finding new sources of these nutrients is a crucial issue. "The general conundrum we somehow need to solve is: Where do we get the appropriate amounts of protein for a still-growing global population without the big environmental footprint?" says Monika Zurek, a food systems scientist at the University of Oxford, who was not involved in the new research. Humans' dietary staples, particularly those of Westerners, have serious consequences. The environmental impacts of cattle products such as beef are especially costly: the animals produce nearly 10 percent of the world's greenhouse gas emissions, and growing food for them spurs deforestation. Pork brings a separate set of environmental hazards, notably water pollution from pig waste. The chicken industry faces similar issues.

But how do you get from the challenge of providing sufficient protein to farming pythons for meat? For Dan Natusch, a herpetologist at Macquarie University in Australia, the idea came about tangentially. He and his colleagues were working with existing commercial python farms in Vietnam and Thailand to determine whether they could distinguish wild-bred snakes from captive-bred ones. During the study, the researchers noticed the farmed pythons' propensity for speedy growth, which they've documented in research published in *Scientific Reports* on March 14.

"As snake biologists, we already knew that pythons had impressive physiologies," Natusch says. "After speaking with the python farmers and continuing to monitor their growth rates, their remarkable physiologies became even more apparent."

Part of the explanation boils down to biology. Pythons, like all snakes, are ectotherms, or cold-blooded animals, which means their body temperature is controlled by their surroundings. This lifestyle makes snakes prone to sunbathing, but it also means that, unlike mammals, ectotherms don't need to produce heat to keep themselves warm–a major source of energy savings that allows them to efficiently convert food into body mass.

Natusch and his colleagues decided to quantify that efficiency. The team studied reticulated pythons (*Malayopython reticulatus*) and Burmese pythons (*Python bivittatus*) on the farms, analyzing what they ate and how quickly they grew.

In particular, the researchers were struck by the pythons' resilience during long fasts: the animals sometimes went months without eating but also without losing much weight. "Observing the ability of relatively young snakes to go many months without food and remain in a healthy state with minimal loss of body condition was really astounding," Natusch says. Notably, he and his colleagues think that such resilience could be valuable during a major disruption to the food system, such as what occurred during the early days of the COVID pandemic, when some farmers couldn't afford to keep feeding their livestock but also couldn't get them to processors.

"Because we expect even greater global economic and climatic volatility in [the] future, pythons could be a solution for those future challenges," Natusch says. "Farming pythons could be a big part of the solution for a part of the world that is already suffering from severe protein deficiency," such as Africa.

Yet Zurek says it's too early to bet on snakes, despite their impressive metabolic feats, to revolutionize our food systems. She sees a need for many more studies about pythons–especially detailed analyses of the environmental impact of farming them and of their nutritional content, including both proteins and micronutrients.

"The current study opens up an interesting step in that direction, but you need to complement that with a whole bunch of additional studies to look at these other aspects before you can really say, 'Yeah, that's an option,'" Zurek says.

And of course, it all depends on whether people will take to eating python. Natusch says python meat is "pretty tasty and versatile" and argues that by his tally, a billion people in Southeast and East Asia, as well as parts of Latin America and Africa, already consider snake meat a culturally acceptable food. "It is really just Western cultures (which have few naturally occurring large reptiles) that haven't been exposed to it," he says.

About the Author

Meghan Bartels is a science journalist based in New York City. She joined Scientific American *in 2023 and is now a senior news reporter there. Previously, she spent more than four years as a writer and editor at Space.com, as well as nearly a year as a science reporter at* Newsweek, *where she focused on space and Earth science. Her writing has also appeared in* Audubon, Nautilus, Astronomy *and* Smithsonian, *among other publications. She attended Georgetown University and earned a master's degree in journalism at New York University's Science, Health and Environmental Reporting Program.*

Massively Reducing Food Waste Could Feed the World

By Chad Frischmann & Mamta Mehra

Imagine going to the market, leaving with three full bags of groceries and coming home. Before you step through your door, you stop and throw one of the bags into a trash bin, which later is hauled away to a landfill. What a waste. Collectively, that is exactly what we are doing today. Globally, 30 to 40 percent of food intended for human consumption is not eaten. Given that more than 800 million people go hungry every day, the scale of food loss fills many of us with a deep sense of anguish.

If population growth and economic development continue at their current pace, the world will have to produce 53 million more metric tons of food annually by 2050. That increase would require converting another 442 million hectares of forests and grassland–far greater than the size of India–into farmland over the next 30 years. The escalation would also release the equivalent of an additional 80 billion tons of carbon dioxide over the next 30 years–about 15 times the emissions of the entire U.S. economy in 2019. Food waste already accounts for roughly 8 percent of the world's greenhouse gases.

There is another path, however. Our group at Project Drawdown, an international research and communications organization, completed an exhaustive study of existing technologies and practices that can significantly reduce greenhouse gas levels in the atmosphere while ushering in a more regenerative society and economy. Reducing food waste is one of the top-five means of achieving these goals among 76 we analyzed. Basic adjustments in how food is produced and consumed could help feed the entire world a healthy, nutrient-rich diet through 2050 and beyond without clearing, planting or grazing more land than is used today. Providing more food by eliminating waste, along with better ways of producing that food, would avoid deforestation and also save an enormous amount of energy, water, fertilizer, labor and other resources.

Opportunities to reduce waste exist at every step along the supply chain from farm to table. We harvest crops, raise livestock, and process these commodities into products such as rice, vegetable oil, potato chips, perfectly cut carrots, cheese and New York strip steaks. Most of these products are packaged in cardboard boxes, plastic bags and bottles, tin cans and glass jars made from extracted materials in industrial factories, and then they are shipped on gas-guzzling trucks, trains and planes all over the world.

After arriving at stores and restaurants, food is held in energy-hungry refrigerators and freezers that use hydrofluorocarbons—powerful greenhouse gases—until purchased by consumers, whose eyes are often bigger than their appetites, particularly in richer communities. In high-income countries, restaurants and households turn on their energy-consuming stoves and ovens, and in developing nations, billions of people burn biomass in noxious cookstoves that spew polluting, unhealthy smoke and black carbon.

After all these waste-producing activities, too much of the food that makes it to a consumer's table is thrown in the garbage, which then is typically transported by fossil-fueled trucks to landfills where it decomposes and emits methane, another potent greenhouse gas. Tossing that leftover lasagna accounts for far more emissions than a rotting tomato that never leaves the farm gate. We can do better.

Smaller Foodprint

At Project Drawdown, we poured global data from the Food and Agriculture Organization and many other sources into a detailed model of the entire food production and consumption system. The model took into account rising population projections, as well as greater consumption and more meat eating per person, particularly in developing countries, based on actual trends over the past several decades. According to our calculations, healthier diets and more regenerative agricultural production lead to a lower "foodprint"–less waste, fewer emissions and a cleaner environment.

If half of the world's population consumes a healthy 2,300 kilocalories a day, built around a plant-rich diet, and puts into practice already proven actions that cut waste across the supply chain, food losses could decline from the current 40 percent to 20 percent, an incredible savings. If we were even more ambitious in following the same practices, food waste could be cut to 10 percent.

These hefty savings would result partly from shifts in basic habits. In the developed world, embracing an average daily 2,300-kilocalorie diet instead of consumption that often reaches more than 3,000 kilocalories lessens food waste in the first place. In the developing world, caloric and protein intake generally need to rise to reach nutritious levels, which may increase some waste across the system. But overall, if everyone on the planet adopted healthy consumption practices and a plant-rich (not necessarily vegetarian) diet, 166 million metric tons of food waste could be avoided over the next 30 years. Feedback would be sent across the supply chain to increase crop production and decrease animal production.

Reducing waste by adjusting how food is produced and consumed can greatly help the environment as well. Different types of foods such as grains, vegetables, fish, meat and dairy have very different environmental footprints. On average, growing and harvesting one kilogram of tomatoes creates about 0.35 kilogram of carbon dioxide emissions. Producing the same amount of beef creates an average of 36 kilograms of emissions. With the entire supply chain taken into account, greenhouse gas emissions from plant-based commodities are 10 to 50 times lower than from most animal-based products.

Additionally, industrial agriculture has spread monocropping, excessive tillage, and widespread use of synthetic fertilizers and pesticides. These practices degrade soil and emit a vast amount of greenhouse gases. Staples are still destroyed in the field by pests and disease and can rot in storage. Livestock consumption of grasses and feed adds further emissions.

Agroecological pest-management practices, such as planting different crops together, and smarter crop rotation can suppress pests and weeds, reducing these losses. Improved livestock-management practices, such as silvopasture, which integrates trees into foraging land, can improve the quality and quantity of animal-based products: more food from fewer hooves in the field and thus fewer resources used and fewer losses. And because regenerative farming practices—which can increase yield from 5 to 35 percent, restore soils and pull more carbon from the air—use compost and manure instead of artificial fertilizers, any food that fails to leave the farm gate can be recycled as natural fertilizer or can be converted by anaerobic digesters into biogas for energy on the farm. More farms need to convert to such practices. Restaurants across the U.S. are helping them through one interesting organization called Zero Foodprint, started by chef Anthony Myint, which takes a few cents added to patrons' bills to fund regenerative farms in the making.

Saving the Third Bag

In low-income countries, most food is lost before ever getting to market. Improving education and professional training for farmers and producers there, along with innovative technologies, can minimize waste. India's state of Jharkhand, for example, has installed solar-powered refrigeration units that allow farmers who produce vegetables, fruits and other perishables to store their products without sacrificing quality—a project led by the United Nations Development Program and the Global Environment Facility. In Africa, the Consortium of International Agricultural Research Centers has expanded training that will help local farmers grow more food under conditions being created by climate change, using crops that better tolerate drought and no-till farming to protect withering soil.

In high- and medium-income countries, most waste occurs at the end of the supply chain—markets and households. There consumers have a tremendous amount of power to prevent waste. A good first step is to reflect on what and how much we are buying. This begins with conscious decisions to purchase what we intend to eat and to eat what we purchase. Rather than overstocking on perishables and other products, buying appropriate quantities of food reduces waste. If too much is cooked for the dinner table, properly storing leftovers reduces spoilage, or they can be shared with neighbors, building stronger community ties.

Broader cultural shifts are also required. The "inglorious fruits and vegetables" campaign launched by the French supermarket chain Intermarché in 2014 aimed to avoid waste by changing cultural attitudes toward "imperfect" foods. Markets tend to procure only fruits and vegetables that meet an idealized cultural perception of shape and color. Imperfect produce that does not match these false traits accounts for up to 40 percent of edible fruits and vegetables being discarded before they leave the farm gate. Instead Intermarché sells these fruits and vegetables in special aisles and runs a national marketing campaign glorifying the inglorious. Other retailers are going even further: All the shelves at Danish supermarket WeFood are stocked with products that would have gone to a landfill. Pittsburgh-based 412 Food Rescue distributes nutritious food that was destined for landfills because of imperfections, limited freshness (such as day-old bread) and unclear labeling to communities in need–for free.

Wholesalers, retailers and restaurants can play a significant role in shrinking the waste piles. They can demand that suppliers use more food from local regenerative farms. Ensuring that food items are sold with clear, standardized "sell by/use by" labels helps store managers know when to mark down items, and it helps consumers know when and when not to dispose of food. Restaurant owners can offer different portion sizes and fewer menu items and can encourage patrons to take leftovers home.

Governments and companies that offer food services to employees can jump in, too. U.S. federal government cafeterias serve more than two million people; imagine if the kitchen managers chose to offer plant-rich fare made from perfectly imperfect produce procured from regenerative suppliers. Google is already doing more of that in its cafeterias today.

No matter how conscientious we all are, some food will inevitably be lost across the supply chain. Anaerobic digesters and composting are better ways of disposal than dumping food in landfills because they create soil or generate electricity. Nine states across the U.S. now have laws requiring that organic waste be diverted from landfills to avoid potent methane emissions. The latest Project Drawdown analysis shows that implementing these solutions globally can reduce greenhouse gas emissions by around 14 billion metric tons over the next 30 years.

The real magic happens when a variety of solutions are adopted in parallel and sustained over time. The decisions people make as farmers, executives, grocers, chefs and consumers can prevent enough food loss to feed the world through 2050 without converting any more land. That means together we can eliminate hunger and support a healthier global population. And there would still be enough cropland available to grow plants for organic materials such as bioplastics, insulation and biofuels.

Revamping the food chain and adjusting eating habits will not happen overnight. Nor should we expect to immediately become perfect, regeneratively minded, plant-rich connoisseurs who are fastidious about our purchases and what we waste. Our most fundamental task is to be conscientious about the choices we make—to try to be "solutionists" as much as we can. Together we can save that third bag of groceries.

About the Authors

Chad Frischmann is co-author, lead researcher and creator of the Drawdown Solutions Framework at Project Drawdown, an international research group focused on solving climate change.

Mamta Mehra is a senior fellow for the land-use and food sectors at Project Drawdown.

Spray-On, Rinse-Off Food 'Wrapper' Can Cut Plastic Packaging

By Sam Jones

Packaging is essential for preserving and distributing many kinds of foods, but it often incorporates plastic–scraps of which already litter too much of the planet, posing a threat to wildlife and contaminating drinking water and soil. Now researchers say they have developed a nontoxic, biodegradable and antimicrobial food coating that could reduce food waste and foodborne illness without adding plastic to the environment. A new study shows this material can be effectively sprayed on individual pieces of produce, such as fruits or vegetables. Removing it is as simple as rinsing it off with water.

Protecting edible items from bacteria and other microorganisms reduces spoilage, which is a major factor in food being tossed out. And this kind of waste is a root cause of worldwide hunger: every year roughly one third of food produced across the globe goes to waste. That's not the only reason to shield produce from germs–some microorganisms are also the sources of illnesses, including listeriosis and *Escherichia coli* poisoning. Foodborne illnesses cause more than 420,000 estimated deaths worldwide annually.

Unfortunately, packing food to preserve it also adds massively to environmental plastic. "Food packaging is definitely enemy number one when it comes to plastic pollution," says Win Cowger, an environmental scientist at the Moore Institute for Plastic Pollution Research, who was not involved in the new study. "We can see globally that food packaging is the most abundant plastic material in the environment." Although the new coating would only replace a portion of the packaging out there–it would not touch some of the greatest offenders, such as water bottles and coffee cup lids–Cowger says any step toward reducing plastic pollution is a good one.

Plastics can stick around in the environment for a long time—potentially forever—but the new coating is biodegradable. That's because of its primary ingredient: pullulan, an edible fiber that is "generally recognized as safe" (GRAS) by the U.S. Food and Drug Administration. The coating also incorporates the naturally derived antimicrobial agents citric acid and thyme oil, as well as a bacterially produced compound called nisin, all of which are widely deemed safe for human consumption in the amounts involved. It is described in a new study published this week in *Nature Food*.

The study researchers used a manufacturing system called focused rotary jet spinning, or FRJS, to generate antimicrobial-laced fibers and apply them to food. Harvard University bioengineer and study co-author Huibin Chang compares the FRJS system to a cotton candy machine, which rapidly spins melted sugar to drive it through small holes, producing fine strands that can be wrapped around a paper cone. FRJS also creates a focused stream of gossamer fibers (made of pullulan in this case rather than flavored sugar) that can be wrapped around a food item—an avocado, for instance. But FRJS—developed in study co-author and bioengineer Kit Parker's Harvard lab, where Chang is a researcher—was not originally designed for food applications. "When we created this technology, we used it for tissue engineering," Chang says. For example, he explains, FRJS played a role in his previous work building three-dimensional models of certain heart structures.

The researchers tested the coating on avocados because these fruits are especially prone to uneven ripening and postharvest decay. After being deposited on an avocado via FRJS, the nontoxic pullulan coating could be easily rinsed off in a sink and washed down the drain, the study found. "You can package the avocado at the farm and extend the shelf life, and then you can wash the coating away," says study co-author Philip Demokritou, a nanoaerosol researcher at Rutgers University and Harvard. Even if the treated object itself is discarded, its coating will degrade in soil in about three days, according to the scientists.

The team also tested how much the coating improved food safety. When the researchers pitted it against common foodborne pathogens, including *E. coli*, *Listeria innocua* and *Aspergillus fumigatus*, they saw a reduction in both bacterial and fungal populations. They also found that avocados with the coating were less likely to rot: just 50 percent of these fruits went bad over the course of a week, compared with 90 percent of the uncoated produce. And the coated avocados were more likely to retain their green internal color.

Although this is not the first antimicrobial food coating, the researchers believe they have created the most effective and easily disposed of option to date. They contend that the spray-on technology requires less starting material, making it more efficient than silk-fiber-based coatings, which require that food first be dipped in the material and then dried. Other attempts at plastic-free food packaging have involved cellulose-based films; these cannot be rinsed off and some even need to be recycled.

The team is currently working on scaling up the coating process to treat multiple pieces of produce at once, Chang says. The scientists are considering several options, including an assembly-line-based system, but this is still in the early stages of planning.

The coating may also need to undergo further safety testing, suggests Nishad Jayasundara, an environmental toxicologist at Duke University, who was not involved with the study. "As a toxicologist," he says, "the primary thought whenever you see a newly synthesized product is 'Do we know enough about it?'" For instance, although the coating's starting materials are nontoxic, washing them down the drain could make them break down into unexpected by-products.

Jayasundara says he is generally encouraged by the new study results. "It's always very exciting when you have biodegradable material that can replace or reduce plastics at any level possible," he says. But he is hesitant to celebrate just yet. Although the FDA has given pullulan the agency's GRAS designation, Jayasundara cautions that whenever there are modifications to a material—even with natural additives such as the antimicrobials the researchers used–it is important to evaluate their safety to human health using a range of tests.

"When we first thought about plastics, they were deemed pretty safe molecules," Jayasundara notes. "But over time we realized, 'Oh, actually, no, that's not the case.' Now we know that plastics at all levels, regardless of the size, have cellular-level effects, molecular-level effects and ecosystem-level effects."

About the Author

Sam Jones is a biomedical scientist turned science writer, editor and producer based in Washington, D.C.

Here's How Much Food Contributes to Climate Change

By Andrea Thompson

As with most things related to people, the food we eat comes with a carbon cost. Soil tillage, crop and livestock transportation, manure management and all the other aspects of global food production generate greenhouse gas emissions to the tune of more than 17 billion metric tons per year, according to a new study published on Monday in *Nature Food*. Animal-based foods account for 57 percent of those emissions, and plant-based ones make up 29 percent. The researchers hope the paper's detailed breakdown of how much each agricultural practice, animal product, crop and country contributes to carbon emissions can help focus and fine-tune reduction efforts.

Though previous studies have estimated emissions from agriculture, the authors say this work is more detailed and comprehensive. It uses data on 171 crops and 16 animal products from more than 200 countries, along with computer modeling, to calculate the amounts of carbon dioxide, methane and nitrous oxide that are contributed by individual elements of the global food system, including consumption and production. If we want to control those emissions, "we needed to calculate a good baseline," says study co-author Atul Jain, a climate scientist at the University of Illinois at Urbana-Champaign.

The results align with other research, says Liqing Peng, a food and agriculture modeler at the nonprofit World Resources Institute, which published its own report on agricultural emissions in 2019. The new study's estimate of total emissions is on the higher side of the range of previous ones, she says. This is partly because it includes data on farmland management practices, such as irrigation and planting, as well as activities beyond the farm, such as processing and packaging–numbers which are difficult to obtain. "It's really important to get as detailed as possible on these breakdowns" in order to know where to concentrate emissions-reduction research and policies, Peng adds.

Of the food products the study examined, beef production was the top emissions contributor by a wide margin, accounting for 25 percent of the total. Among animal-based products, it was followed by cow milk, pork and chicken meat, in that order. In the category of crops, rice farming was the top contributor–and it was the second-highest contributor among all products, accounting for 12 percent of the total. Rice's relatively high ranking comes from the methane-producing bacteria that thrive in the anaerobic conditions of flooded paddies. After rice, the highest emissions associated with plant production came from wheat, sugarcane and maize.

As for contributions from individual regions, South and Southeast Asia comprised the overall top emitter of greenhouse gases related to food production and the only region where plant-based emissions were higher than animal-based ones because of rice cultivation. Among countries, China, India and Indonesia had the highest plant-based food production emissions. This, again, was linked to rice farming, as well as large populations that create a high demand for food–which drives more conversion of land to agricultural production. Because of their large populations, these areas registered relatively low per capita production emissions. The highest per capita emissions (and the second-highest regional emissions overall) were found in South America because of its relatively large production of meat, particularly beef. North America had the second-highest per capita production emissions, followed by Europe.

The study also broke down emissions caused by various aspects of food production and consumption. Farm activities, such as plowing soil or using other types of equipment–along with the conversion of land from forests or other natural landscapes into pasture and cropland–collectively accounted for two thirds of emissions.

Jain and his colleagues want to use these results, along with computer modeling, to examine how changing farmland management (reducing fertilizer use or employing no-till soil methods, for example) could reduce emissions. They also want to study how to balance the food requirements of a growing global population with the need to halt deforestation. "That's why we put so much effort" into being so comprehensive in the new paper's accounting, Jain says. His co-author Xiaoming Xu, also at the University of Illinois at Urbana-Champaign, is optimistic about the prospects of making a dent in food-based emissions. "I think there are a lot of options we can do," he says. But Peng notes that meeting the current–and ambitious–international emissions-reduction targets will mean figuring out which approaches not only make the most economic sense but also provide the biggest bang for the buck in terms of getting results. "You want to do everything," she says, "but you can't do everything at the same time."

About the author

Andrea Thompson is an associate editor covering the environment, energy and earth sciences. She has been covering these issues for 16 years. Prior to joining Scientific American, *she was a senior writer covering climate science at* Climate Central *and a reporter and editor at* Live Science, *where she primarily covered earth science and the environment. She has moderated panels, including as part of the United Nations Sustainable Development Media Zone, and appeared in radio and television interviews on major networks. She holds a graduate degree in science, health and environmental reporting from New York University, as well as a B.S. and an M.S. in atmospheric chemistry from the Georgia Institute of Technology. Follow Thompson on Bluesky @andreatweather.bsky.social*

How to Make Urban Agriculture More Climate-Friendly

By Joanna Thompson

Stroll through any trendy neighborhood of Brooklyn, N.Y., and you'll notice little pockets of green tucked between the concrete and brownstones. Many of these miniature oases are community gardens, spaces dedicated to growing produce ranging from kale to squash to tomatoes right in the heart of the city. Such projects are often seen as a climate solution—a way to enjoy fresh, local food with minimal environmental impact. But though these spaces have many upsides, reducing carbon emissions isn't always one of them.

A new study in *Nature Cities* compared carbon emissions from small farms and gardens in major cities across the U.S. and Europe with those of a typical industrial farm. The results may surprise many climate-conscious and well-meaning urbanites: per serving of produce, the carbon cost of low-tech urban farms can be up to six times greater than that of industrial farming operations. "We knew it would be high, but we didn't realize it would be *so* high," says study co-author Joshua Newell, a sustainable development researcher at the University of Michigan.

But the process of growing food in cities doesn't have to be so carbon-intensive, Newell says. In fact, when done right, it could have huge environmental and societal benefits—and many researchers still see it as an important part of a more sustainable future.

Urban agriculture—whether it describes towering, high-tech vertical gardens or a small patch of dirt with a few basil plants—has become increasingly popular around the world as food movements such as eating local produce and growing organic crops have gained momentum. These operations are often viewed as a sustainable, community-focused alternative to big industrial farms. But until recently, few studies actually looked at their environmental impact.

Newell and his team decided it was time to change that. Using data from 73 low-tech city farms, community gardens and personal plots of land, they measured the average carbon emissions from growing a single serving of urban produce (say, one medium potato) against the carbon released by growing the equivalent on a conventional commercial farm. The team found that because of urban gardens' relatively low yields, along with the energy used in constructing the planting beds, big-city spuds were significantly more carbon-intensive than commercially grown ones. This held true even when the researchers factored in emissions from transporting commercially grown produce to often distant grocery stores. "Just because it's local doesn't mean it has a lower carbon footprint," Newell says.

One person who wasn't surprised by these results was Carolyn Dimitri, a New York University applied economist, who studies food systems but wasn't involved with the new work. Small, scattered urban plots can't compete with industrial farms in terms of output, she says. Proportionally, it takes a lot more fertilizer, water and new infrastructure to grow a serving of vegetables in a relatively tiny urban space, compared with a conventional farm, which is already designed for high yields. That massive difference in scale and optimization accounts for most of the carbon discrepancies.

That doesn't mean that growing vegetables in big cities is inherently bad, however. "Urban farming is great," if imperfect, says Carola Grebitus, a sociologist specializing in food choice at Arizona State University. It can be a powerful tool for education and job creation, she says, and a good way to introduce fresh produce to urban "food deserts" where healthy fruits and vegetables are hard to come by. Community gardens can also provide a psychologically beneficial place to connect with nature, and the added green space can help mitigate dangerous heat and flooding.

Conscious of these benefits, Newell's team highlighted a number of ways to make urban agriculture more sustainable from a climate perspective. One option is to be selective about what crops are grown. Tomatoes grown in the city, for instance, have a carbon footprint equal to or lower than their industrially farmed counterparts. That's because most commercially produced tomatoes start life in the greenhouse—a resource- and energy-intensive farming method. And a few other highly perishable crops that need to be refrigerated right away, such as asparagus and herbs, have about the same carbon footprint whether they're grown in urban or industrial farm settings.

Another strategy is to rely on existing infrastructure as much as possible. Nearly two-thirds of the carbon emissions from urban agriculture came from operations related to infrastructure, including the demolition and remodeling of old buildings rather than the incorporation of these structures into a new garden's design. The equipment needed to demolish an old building, not to mention a building's original construction, can emit a lot of carbon. Finally, Newell says, any urban farm should take the local climate, water quality and soil into account. Growing plants that are ill-suited to an area requires more water, energy and pesticides, all of which take an environmental toll. Oranges won't thrive in New York City, for example, but they can bear lots of fruit under the hot Phoenix sun.

For Dimitri, this study represents an important step in opening up a more nuanced discussion about urban agriculture. She hopes that future research will highlight even more of the distinctions between commercial farms and urban gardens in different locations. "A farm in Germany is not the same as a farm in the U.S.," she says. "So it would be nice to see maybe country-by-country discussions."

Rather than a one-size-fits-all climate solution, perhaps it is best to view urban farming as something as unique as the vibrant metropolises it is practiced in—each plot as different from others as Munich is from Detroit or New York City is from Paris.

About the Author

Joanna Thompson is an insect enthusiast and former Scientific American *intern. She is based in New York City. Follow Thompson on Twitter @jojofoshosho0*

A Meatless Diet Is Better for You—And the Planet

By Sarah C. Hull

The idea that we need to eat meat to get enough protein and iron, a false assumption of some Paleo diet acolytes, is a common misconception. It ignores the abundance of protein and iron in many plant-based foods such as nuts, seeds and legumes. Similarly, consuming dairy is not necessary to obtain adequate dietary calcium, as this mineral is abundant in soy, lentils, beans, nuts, seeds, grains, leafy greens and cruciferous vegetables.

Likewise, while we typically associate omega-3 fatty acids with fish, fish themselves incorporate these into their tissue by eating algae and seaweed, which we can consume directly without the concerns of exposure to accumulated mercury and microplastics in fish flesh. Indeed, a whole-food, plant-based diet can provide all essential nutrients except for vitamin B12, which is made by bacteria in soil and ingested by animals, thereby incorporated into their tissue, milk, and eggs. While modern sanitation allows humans to consume clean produce uncontaminated by dirt or feces, we can easily and cheaply obtain oral B12 supplements.

Furthermore, significantly reducing our consumption of meat would carry vast benefits. As cardiovascular disease remains the leading cause of death around the world, poor diet has now surpassed tobacco smoking as the top risk factor for death in the U.S, where life expectancy has now stagnated, in large part because of a plateau in mortality from cardiovascular disease. Eating highly processed foods and red meat has been repeatedly demonstrated to promote underlying mechanisms of cancer and cardiovascular disease, such as inflammation and damage to the lining of blood vessels.

Mounting evidence points to the benefits of a whole-food, plant-based diet. A meta-analysis of scientific studies from 2017 found that a vegetarian diet is associated with a 25 percent relative risk reduction for coronary heart disease and an 8 percent relative risk reduction for cancer, with a vegan diet conferring a 15 percent relative risk reduction for cancer. The World Health Organization (WHO) has classified processed meat as carcinogenic, and (unprocessed) red meat as probably carcinogenic to humans. Finally, randomized controlled trials have also demonstrated the benefits of a Mediterranean diet (essentially a whole-food, plant-predominant diet) in both the primary and secondary prevention of cardiovascular disease, with enhanced benefits from greater adherence to a provegetarian (more plant-based) dietary pattern.

In addition to harming ourselves, eating meat harms others. Factory farming practices often entail unspeakable cruelty to animals, and working conditions for human laborers are often unsafe and inhumane as well. Overcrowding of livestock and workers promotes the spread of disease among both people and animals, putting us all at risk for future pandemics. The overuse of "routine" antibiotics to accelerate animal growth and preemptively treat the infections anticipated as a result of living in unclean and overcrowded conditions can promote antibiotic resistance. Finally, meat consumption contributes to climate change though deforestation and methane emissions. Food systems make up a third of global greenhouse gas emissions caused by human activity, and animal-based foods contribute twice the emissions of plant-based foods. Switching from the typical Western diet to a vegetarian diet can reduce one's personal dietary carbon emissions by 30 percent; a strict vegan diet can reduce them by as much as 85 percent.

While large-scale, well-coordinated national and international action is undoubtedly needed to fight both climate change and unscrupulous factory farming practices—and to ensure the availability of nutritious and healthy food for all citizens regardless of zip code, educational attainment or financial resources—this should not be an excuse for individuals to resist implementing change in their own lives and communities. Societies change when enough individuals within them alter their behavior, and it is up to each of us to act as a change agent in whatever capacity we can. Those with more limited means may only be capable of small incremental modifications to their lifestyle, such as committing to avoiding meat one day out of the week ("Meatless Mondays") or considering a "flexitarian" approach to meal planning that decenters meat as the focal point of meals. Even modest reductions in meat consumption and progress toward a more plant-forward diet can yield significant health and environmental benefits, particularly when applied on the population level.

Those with greater influence, such as physicians, educators and policy makers, should consider the importance of acting as role models for healthy behaviors themselves as well as advocating for policies that ensure better nutritional access and education for others. According to the EAT-Lancet Commission, which issued a 2019 report on globally sustainable diets: "Food is the single strongest lever to optimize human health and environmental sustainability on Earth." While we should continue to push governments and organizations to enact meaningful change in this direction, we would be well served to pull this lever in our own lives as well.

This is an opinion and analysis article, and the views expressed by the author or authors are not necessarily those of Scientific American.

About the Author

Sarah C. Hull is an assistant professor of medicine (cardiology) at the Yale School of Medicine, where she also serves as associate director of the Program for Biomedical Ethics.

How Chocolate Can Help Save the Planet

By Timothy Pearson

You can count on the fact that chocolate will, as always, be a mainstay of Valentine's Day. You can also count on the fact that cocoa bean cultivation is bad for the environment–especially for the rain forests of West Africa. That, along with concerns over child labor on cacao plantations is enough to make the conscientious consumer think about giving up chocolate for good.

But what if we could indulge in chocolate without guilt? Or at least, without climate guilt? In fact, we can, because when cocoa is grown sustainably, it can actually help *save* the world, not destroy it.

Cocoa beans grow in pods on shrubby evergreens that are often planted in the open but can also thrive under canopies of large rainforest trees. A well-managed grove of shade-grown cacao trees can store a significantly higher amount of carbon than maize or other annual crops–up to 150 metric tons per hectare compared with 10 or less for maize–and up to three times the amount stored by cocoa grown in full sun.

Shade-grown cacao trees are also more drought-tolerant and weed-resistant than those grown in the open. They are more friendly to wildlife, creating corridors between forests and enhancing biodiversity. And they provide a way for some of the world's poorest populations to make a living, sustainably.

The problem is not that cacao trees can't help the environment. The problem is that too few of them do. The reasons for this are complex, but mainly boil down to lack of resources, lack of information and insecure land tenure.

Many West African cacao farmers are sharecroppers. They can't remove old, diseased trees because this would jeopardize the tenuous hold they have on the land. They can't afford to plant new trees, either. As a result new cacao farms are usually created by entrepreneurs who cut down trees and create chemical-intensive monoculture plantations, which both pollute and reduce biodiversity.

As the planet grows warmer and dryer, though, these high-yielding, full-sun cacao varieties are withering in the heat and succumbing to diseases and pests. Many of the small cocoa farms in West Africa's Cocoa belt, which extends from Ivory Coast to Cameroon and supplies up to 70 percent of the world's cocoa, now suffer from low productivity.

But there is hope. When cost and land tenure issues are surmounted, farmers are more than willing to grow resilient cacao in the shade. For instance, when farmers receive help in obtaining the right to farm the land they work, they have the security to improve their groves. That, along with access to finance, means they can replace older trees with more resilient hybrids. Lasting success flows from strategies that protect trees and improve livelihoods.

The cacao tree isn't the only thing that thrives in forests. People do, too. Many of the poorest and most marginalized people in the world–a fifth of the global population–live in forests or on the edges of them. These people need trees for food or fuel or housing. They earn their living from them.

We can't put a fence around forests to keep poor people from exploiting them. Doing so may reduce greenhouse gas emissions, but it's not realistic. We need to fashion a future where forests can be used to benefit those who count on trees for their living without inflicting damage on the rest of the planet. And in the cacao groves of West Africa where these conditions are being met, plants and people are thriving.

Trees are crucial weapons in the fight against climate change, but they're also vital to the livelihoods of 1.5 billion people, including those of cocoa farmers. So enjoy your chocolate–provided that it's a sustainable, shade-grown brand. In fact, buy, eat and give as much of it as you like. Your sweetheart will thank you. The world will, too.

This article was published in Scientific American's *former blog network and reflects the views of the author, not necessarily those of* Scientific American.

About the author

Timothy Pearson is a carbon specialist who directs the Ecosystem Services Unit at the nonprofit Winrock International and a lead author and technical expert for the new global emissions reduction verification system Architecture for REDD+ Transactions (ART).

GLOSSARY

bariatric Relating to the treatment of obesity.

cardiovascular Relating to the heart and blood vessels.

cultivate To foster the growth of plants.

denature To alter the molecular structure of a substance.

fermentation In food and drink, the action of breaking down a substance with the aid of microorganisms.

food desert An area where humans live but there is a lack of nearby, affordable grocery stores and restaurants.

genetically modified organism (GMO) A plant or animal whose DNA has been changed.

grafting The act of propagating a plant by combining it with another plant.

hominid A group of erect mammals that includes modern humans, ancestral humans, and extinct and existing great apes.

hydroponics The process of growing plants without soil.

metabolism The way in which a living body processes a substance, especially food.

microbiome Microorganisms that live in a particular environment in the human body.

monoclonal antibody An antibody created by cloning a single white blood cell.

neurotransmitter A molecule that acts as a chemical messenger in the body.

pasteurization The act of sterilizing a liquid such as milk.

pathogen A substance that causes disease.

radiocarbon dating The act of determining the age of something by studying its chemical components.

satiety The state of feeling satisfied or full from eating.

sommelier A person who is an expert on wine.

FURTHER INFORMATION

Bourzac, Katherine. "61 Unexpected 'Forever Chemicals' Found in Food Packaging," *Scientific American*, March 19, 2024, www.scientificamerican.com/article/61-unexpected-pfas-forever-chemicals-found-in-food-packaging.

Damman, Christopher. "What If You Could Rank Food By 'Healthiness' as You Shopped? Nutrient Profiling Systems Use Algorithms to Simplify Picking Healthy Groceries," *The Conversation*, December 26, 2024, theconversation.com/what-if-you-could-rank-food-by-healthiness-as-you-shopped-nutrient-profiling-systems-use-algorithms-to-simplify-picking-healthy-groceries-245844.

Denworth, Lydia. "Delicious Bacon Highlights Food That Enraptures Our Senses but Endangers Our Health," *Scientific American*, December 17, 2024, www.scientificamerican.com/article/delicious-bacon-highlights-food-that-enraptures-our-senses-but-endangers-our-health.

Garza, Frida. "How Food Banks Prevented 1.8 Million Metric Tons of Carbon Emissions Last Year," *Grist*, August 15, 2024, sentientmedia.org/food-banks-prevented-carbon-emissions.

Gobel, Reyna. "The FDA Is Changing What Foods Can Be Called 'Healthy,'" *Scientific American*, December 27, 2024, www.scientificamerican.com/article/the-fda-is-changing-what-foods-can-be-called-healthy.

Kordas, Katarzyna. "Cinnamon, Spice, and 'Everything Nice'– Why Lead-Tainted Cinnamon Products Have Turned up on Shelves, and What Questions Consumers Should Ask," *The Conversation*, November 27, 2024, theconversation.com/cinnamon-spice-and-everything-nice-why-lead-tainted-cinnamon-products-have-turned-up-on-shelves-and-what-questions-consumers-should-ask-241211.

Wong, Carissa. "Eat Less Meat: Will the First Global Climate Deal on Food Work?" *Nature*, December 8, 2023, www.nature.com/articles/d41586-023-03960-0.

Zeeberg, Amos. "The Processed Food Fight," *OpenMind Magazine*, April 26, 2024, www.openmindmag.org/articles/the-processed-food-fight.

CITATIONS

1.1 The Surprising Story of How Peaches Became an Icon of the U.S. Southwest by Meghan Bartels (October 25, 2024); 1.2 1,800-Year-Old Spices Are Earliest Evidence of Curry Making in Southeast Asia by O. Rose Broderick (July 21, 2023); 1.3 Science Shows Why Traditional Kimchi Making Works So Well by Rachel Crowell (May 16, 2023); 1.4 To Follow the Real Early Human Diet, Eat Everything by Kate Wong (June 25, 2024); 1.5 Gene Variant May Have Helped Ancient Humans Survive Starvation by James Dinneen (January 1, 2022); 1.6 Wine's True Origins Are Finally Revealed by Mark Fischetti and Francesco Franchi (October 1, 2023); 2.1 We Are Living in a Golden Age of Apples by Laura Helmuth (October 24, 2024); 2.2 The Science of Melting Cheese by Meghan Bartels (October 2, 2024); 2.3 Period Food Cravings Are Real. A New Brain Finding Could Explain Why They Happen by Jocelyn Solis-Moreira (September 21, 2023); 2.4 Food Can Be Literally Addictive, New Evidence Suggests by Marta Zaraska (September 11, 2023); 2.5 Your Genes May Influence What You Like to Eat by Lauren J. Young (August 1, 2023); 3.1 Artificial Sweetener Erythritol Linked to Blood Clots, Study Warns by Kate Graham-Shaw (August 22, 2024); 3.2 How to Know if You Have Food Poisoning, And How to Avoid It by Kate Graham-Shaw (August 16, 2024); 3.3 People with Food Allergies Can Treat Symptoms with Asthma Medication, FDA Decides by Andrew Chapman (March 1, 2024); 3.4 Can Coffee's Effects on Appetite and Digestion Cause Weight Loss by Lori Youmshajekian (August 13, 2024); 3.5 Some Sugar Substitutes Affect Blood Glucose and Gut Bacteria by Emily Willingham (August 19, 2022); 3.6 How Do Ultraprocessed Foods Affect Your Health? by Lori Youmshajekian (November 8, 2023); 3.7 Ozempic Quiets Food Noise in the Brain—But How? by Lauren J. Young (June 25, 2024); 4.1 Florida's Beef with Lab-Grown Meat is Evidence-Free by Allison Parshall (May 3, 2024); 4.2 Tweaking Vegetables' Genes Could Make Them Tastier—And You'll Get to Try Them Soon by Meghan Bartels (May 10, 2023); 4.3 Robotic Bees Could Support Vertical Farms Today and Astronauts Tomorrow by Molly Glick (July 17, 2023); 4.4 Why Is It So Hard to Make Vegan Fish? by Joanna Thompson (February 28, 2023); 4.5 Flavor-Enhancing Spoons and Chopsticks Could Make Food Taste Better by Saugat Bolakhe (January 9, 2023); 4.6 Plants Have Hormones, Too, and Tweaking Them Could Improve Food Supply by Sara Reardon (July 30, 2020); 4.7 Breeding a Nonallergenic Peanut by Peter Beetham (November 25, 2019); 5.1 Snake Steak Could Be a Climate-Friendly Source of Protein by Meghan Bartels (March 14, 2024); 5.2 Massively Reducing Food Waste Could Feed the World by Chad Frischmann and Manta Mehra (October 1, 2021); 5.3 Spray-On, Rinse-Off Food 'Wrapper' Can Cut Plastic Packaging by Sam Jones (June 24, 2022); 5.4 Here's How Much Food Contributes to Climate Change by Andrea Thompson (September 13, 2021); 5.5 How to Make Urban Agriculture More Climate-Friendly by Joanna Thompson (February 2, 2024); 5.6 A Meatless Diet Is Better for You—And the Planet by Sarah C. Hull (July 14, 2023); 5.7 How Chocolate Can Help Save the Planet by Timothy Pearson (February 12, 2020).

Each author biography was accurate at the time the article was originally published.

INDEX